Landmark
BOOKS

THE FIRST TRANSATLANTIC CABLE

THE FIRST TRANSATLANTIC CABLE

Adele Gutman Nathan

ILLUSTRATED BY DENVER GILLEN

Random House, New York

First Printing

 Published in New York by Random House, Inc., and simultaneously in Toronto, Canada, by Random House of Canada, Limited.
Library of Congress Catalog Card Number: 59-6471
Manufactured in the United States of America

CONTENTS

What Are *the Facts of History?*

Anybody writing a short, readable account today about the Atlantic cable must choose among the many versions of the great adventure. And who knows what the exact truth is? Even the judges differed in their opinions when lawsuits were started by various people claiming part of the credit for the cable.

But that's the way it is with history, and that's why it's fun to study history.

Before I started writing this book I read the diaries of Cyrus Field, of Daniel Gooch, and of James C. Dean, secretary of the Anglo-American Telegram Company. I read the contemporary reports of the Associated Press, of the New York *Times,* of the London *Times,* of Punch, the English weekly magazine, the logs of several of the cable-laying ships. I read the accounts of Willoughby Smith and Charles Bright which were written later. And I even read many of the court records of the suits about the Atlantic telegraph which, bound into books, are a whole library in themselves. Each told the story in a different way.

So I decided, in writing this version of the laying of the Atlantic cable, that first of all I would try to recreate the flavor of the era. With this in mind I have followed mostly John Mullaly's *The Laying of the Cable,* Sir William Howard Russell's *The Atlantic Telegraph* (both eyewitness accounts), the letters of Professor Morse, the letters of Captain Maury (some of them written to his daughter), the speeches of Cyrus W. Field, the records of the Gutta Percha Company and Glass, Elliot and Company (now all gathered together in the offices of the Telcon Company), and the newspaper stories in the New York and London *Times.*

In some cases I have simplified quotations with the object of making them shorter and more understandable.

I have also used Dr. Henry Field's book, *History of the Atlantic Telegraph,* as a sort of guide. Dr. Field wrote his book as a tribute to his brother. The later editions were published at a time when the question of who really did first think of the Atlantic telegraph was being argued in the courts.

Each of the men who wrote of the great cable gamble told the story in a different way. Each had his own point of view.

And much of the data given out at the time has since been proved to be inaccurate.

A number of years ago I helped install the Communications Room at the Museum of the City of New York. The rare and valuable research material that went into this work is now in the archives of the American Telephone and Telegraph Company, and I was able to use it through the good offices of Walter Gifford, former president of the company, and his tireless secretary, Evelyn G. Betts.

Many manuscripts, early papers and other hard-to-find items were put at my disposal by P. L. Reed, Public Relations Officer of the Telegraph Construction and Maintenance Company, Ltd., of London, Major C. B. Ormerod, C.B.E. and Ruth Isaacs of the British Information Services in New York. Help has also been given me by Jesse Bell of the American Telephone and Telegraph Company, John Rosenburg of the Long Lines Information Department of the same company, George Griswold, Jr., of the Bell Laboratories, and G. D. Collas of British and Irish Railroads. The late Ralph Mooney, former historian of the American Telephone and Telegraph Company, E. T. Mottram of the Bell Laboratories, and James B. Meriwether of Princeton were good enough to read the manuscript and make suggestions.

To all these people and many more, both grownups and young people, whose names I have not set down, I wish to express my gratitude. In addition, I want to thank my research assistants, Lillian Gainsburgh, Hugh Ferrell and Ann Miner. Finally a word of appreciation to my editor, Louise

Bonino, her associate, Walter Retan, and to my literary mentor, Nannine Joseph, whose patience and encouragement have kept me going through the three long years it has taken to finish this book.

ADELE GUTMAN NATHAN

THE FIRST TRANSATLANTIC CABLE

1

Mr. Gisborne Comes to New York

On a cold night in January, 1854, two men sat before a comfortable fire in the ornate library of the New York mansion of Cyrus West Field. One of the men was Mr. Field himself. The other was Frederick N. Gisborne.

Mr. Field was a big man. But he was settled down so far in his high-backed wing chair that his face was in shadow. Mr. Gisborne occupied a much smaller chair opposite, directly under the blazing, many-bracketed gas chandelier overhead.

Mr. Field had placed the chairs that way so he could

watch Mr. Gisborne. This was his way of doing business.

Mr. Field was a typical businessman. At thirty-five he was getting to be a little on the heavy side, and his hands were soft and white. He was dressed in a cutaway coat, a brilliant white collar and stock, an embroidered vest and striped trousers. He parted his hair in the middle and let it grow a little long in back. A curling fringe of chin whiskers extended from ear to ear.

His eyes, under long straight brows, were keen and steady. His nose was big and long enough to smell out a bargain. He could be charming whenever he wished, but just now he had put on the poker face he used for doing business.

Mr. Gisborne looked as if he had spent a great deal of time outdoors. He was about ten years younger than Mr. Field, and very tall and stringy. His tweedy clothes had a backwoods cut. And so did his high-laced boots. His hands were brown and rough. His bristling hair was clipped, and he was clean-shaven except for short sideburns.

Mr. Gisborne sat on the edge of his chair and talked excitedly without trying to hide anything. "All my relatives say I'm a fool and my friends call me a wild man. They think my scheme is just so much poppycock and that I ought to forget it. Maybe they're right. After all, I was doing well as an engineer before this bug bit me. I had a good job in Nova Scotia, working for the telegraph company.

"We were extending the lines through Lower Canada and New Brunswick to Halifax," Mr. Gisborne explained. "I was making good money and I liked the work.

"Then all of a sudden this idea hit me. Why not connect Nova Scotia with Newfoundland by way of Cape Breton Island? Then the wire could run across Newfoundland from Cape Ray to St. John's. Since St. John's is the last port of call for the merchantmen on their way from America to Europe, a direct line from New York would clip two whole days from transatlantic messages.

"The only trouble is," Mr. Gisborne went on, "Newfoundland is a wild place. No maps have ever been made of the country, and there are no roads—not even on the coast. And then there's the question of running a cable under the Gulf of St. Lawrence. It would be the longest submarine cable ever laid. So I began to think, maybe they're right; maybe it *is* a crazy idea."

Mr. Gisborne stopped talking for a moment, hoping for some word of encouragement. But Mr. Field just sat still and waited for him to go on.

"Crazy or not, I had to do it," Gisborne continued. "Four years ago I gave up my job. I went to the Newfoundland legislature and laid my plans on the table. The politicos finally decided it was worth a try. They passed an act authorizing me to go ahead and made a grant of five hundred pounds sterling—about $2,500 in our money. They told me I could use it to make a survey of the proposed line.

"It looked like a lot of money to me. I thought sure I could do it for that."

Mr. Gisborne stopped again. Mr. Field was so quiet that his visitor thought perhaps he had fallen asleep. However, a nod from Mr. Field proved he was still awake, so Gisborne went on with the story.

"I started out on the fourth of September with a crew of six white men. In a couple of days I found out that they weren't up to it. So I let them go, and I got four Indians. Before a week was out, two of the Indians deserted. That left just the three of us but we kept on going.

"We were gone nearly three months. By the time we got back to civilization, we were just about at the end of our strength. But it was worth it. We'd done what we set out to do. We'd made working maps of 350 miles of woods and wilderness where no one but Indians had ever been before.

"Now that this part was done," Gisborne explained, "the Newfoundland legislature decided to let me go ahead and try to string the line. But I had made up my mind that projects like this need more than government help. They have to have the backing of private capital—men who are willing to put their money into something with a future.

"I came to New York and got private capital. Then in the autumn I went out on a small steamer to stretch the first American submarine cable of any length. It was to go across the Northumberland Strait from Prince Edward Island to New Brunswick."

Mr. Gisborne stood up and walked to a large globe which was standing in the corner of the library.

"From here to here, you see," he said, pointing.

Mr. Field came over and looked, but he still didn't say a word.

"Then I planned to run a submarine cable from Cape Ray, Newfoundland, to Cape Breton Island," Mr. Gisborne went on. "The Gulf of the St. Lawrence is at its narrowest right there. I didn't figure it would be much of a job. But the cable broke when we were just a few miles at sea. So we decided to put what money was left into completing the land line."

Mr. Gisborne took a turn or two around the room and then sat down.

Mr. Field stood studying the globe for a moment. Then he, too, went back to his chair.

"From here on the story is just one of failure," said Gisborne at last. "I thought the first surveying trip was rough, but this was twice as bad. We constructed some thirty or forty miles of line, and then the money gave out. What could we do? Bills came in from all sides. I put up everything I had, but after all I'm only a poor engineer. It wasn't anything like enough."

He leaned forward.

"Maybe you won't want to do business with me, Mr. Field," he said, "when you hear what happened next. I was arrested and thrown in jail. After a few months, creditors saw there was nothing to be gained by this, so I was let go. Yesterday I was standing in the Astor House with my hat in my hand once more when I had a stroke of luck. I met Mr. Matthew Field, your brother.

"I found out that he was an engineer. Right away I began telling him about what I'd been doing. Before

I was halfway through, he suggested that I see you. You are the very man, he said, to get behind the Newfoundland telegraph."

Mr. Gisborne had had his say. He sat on the edge of his chair and waited.

"Of course, I appreciate the compliment which my brother has paid me," Mr. Field began cautiously. "But I do not propose to undertake any new projects. I have retired from active commerce. I have just returned

Mr. Field stood for a moment studying the globe.

from a pleasure trip to South America, and I am planning to occupy my time in the future with similar trips. And Mr. Matthew Field knows as well as anyone that I am definitely through with business."

"I wouldn't blame you a bit if you didn't want to do business with a jailbird," Mr. Gisborne began.

But Mr. Field interrupted him. He gave Gisborne one of his warmest smiles.

"There is nothing about your story that is not honorable to you," he said. "I myself once failed in business. But I went to work again, and I'm happy to say I was able to pay off all my creditors. I even made a considerable fortune for myself. It seems to me you have acted most honorably, and with great energy."

Mr. Gisborne sat back in his chair and drew a deep breath. He was over the first hurdle.

"You come to me with a fine recommendation from my brother," Mr. Field went on. "But frankly, as I said to him, all this business of cutting two days from the delivery of transatlantic messages doesn't interest me much. If there were some promise of greater things to come—say, for instance, a cable to Europe——"

"I was afraid to even mention that," interrupted Gisborne. "I was afraid you'd think I was completely crazy. So many people do. There's already been talk in

Newfoundland of a transatlantic cable. And St. John's would certainly be the jumping-off place for such a scheme. We're learning more and more every day about electromagnetic telegraphy. There's no telling what might happen! Mr. Field, this Newfoundland telegraph must be completed."

Mr. Field rose, walked to the corner of the room and pulled the bell rope. This was his way of indicating that the meeting was over. The butler came in with Mr. Gisborne's hat, but Mr. Field himself went to the front door with his visitor.

"Mind you," Mr. Field said, as Gisborne went down the steps, "I make no promises. Day after tomorrow at ten o'clock in the morning, I will meet you at the Astor House. I will invite Mr. Matthew Field and another brother of mine who is a lawyer to be there. And we'll talk further. Good night."

As soon as Mr. Gisborne had left, Mr. Field went back to the library. Once more he began studying the globe. . . . With his finger he made a line from Newfoundland across the great arc to the coast of Ireland.

"A transatlantic cable," he said aloud. "An Atlantic submarine electromagnetic telegraph."

He turned out the gas and went to bed.

2

Under the English Channel

While Frederick Gisborne was trying to string a wire across the wilderness of Newfoundland, John and Jacob Brett, two Englishmen, were grappling with the problem of connecting the British Isles with the Continent by submarine cable.

In the ten years that had passed since Samuel Finley Breese Morse successfully tapped out signals from Washington to Baltimore, the telegraph idea had caught on all over the world.

Telegraph wires crossed national boundaries,

climbed mountains and stretched across rivers. Messages flew back and forth between Rome, Vienna, Madrid, Bern, Moscow, Berlin, Paris and even Bombay in a matter of hours. A whole network of wires covered Britain. The threads ran through Glasgow, Birmingham, Liverpool, Plymouth, London and Dover.

But there was no line connecting London and the other capitals of the world. England was cut off from the mainland by twenty-two miles of stormy, unbridged water—the English Channel. News that could be flashed around Europe was slowed down at the water's edge before it could reach the British Isles.

All sorts of speed-up schemes were tried to close the gap. Every hour news agencies shipped special messengers on small, swift boats between Calais and Dover. Reuters, the wide-awake European news service, flew stock quotations by carrier pigeon from Ostend to Folkestone.

But these were just makeshifts.

Yesterday's news was no longer good enough in this new kind of world.

Then Jacob and John Brett came forward with a scheme for laying a submarine cable between England

and France. The idea took hold of the popular fancy at once.

"Let the lightning be submarinely sent!" screamed the headlines in the London *Times*.

Punch, the London weekly, ran a picture of two ladies designated as "England" and "France." Each carried a palm leaf of peace as they held hands and walked calmly under the English Channel.

The Bretts didn't have too much trouble getting a franchise from the two governments. Then they put up some of their own money and got friends to join them.

The Bretts knew they were taking a big chance. They were in the business of manufacturing wire rope, most of which they sold to land-telegraph companies. They knew from experience that much could go wrong. Land lines were fairly simple—just wires strung from pole to pole. But even those gave plenty of trouble. Any one of a number of things could throw a whole system out of commission.

On land, linesmen could be sent to the trouble spots to repair the damages. But linesmen couldn't go down to the bottom of the sea to mend cables.

There would be other things to contend with. Bare live wires couldn't be put at the bottom of the Channel. There might be sharp rocks down there, for instance. Submarine wires would have to be cushioned against these rocks.

Then there was the question of corrosion caused by water. The cable would have to be waterproofed.

Two kinds of waterproof substances were known at this time. One was India rubber. The other was gutta-percha. Both were made of the gum of trees that grew wild in Malaya. Both were waterproof. And both could be molded when heated.

But rubber still was elastic when it cooled. Vulcanizing (the process of treating rubber with chemicals so that it hardens when cold) had already been invented by Charles Goodyear in America. But he hadn't put it on the market.

So rubber couldn't be used as an insulator.

Cold gutta-percha was hard and black and shiny. It was widely used in England to make a variety of objects, including shoe soles, pipes, skates, picture frames and statues. It was even used for drain pipes.

Gutta-percha was already in use as an insulator on telegraph poles at the points of contact with the live wires. It was known to be a nonconductor.

A German scientist, Werner von Siemens, made a few lengths of insulated cable. He dipped the wire in soft, hot gutta-percha, ran the whole thing through a special machine, and then let it cool. The gutta-percha had hardened but the line was still flexible. He laid his cable under a little river in Germany and transmitted telegrams from bank to bank. He had successfully insulated his wires.

The news of Dr. von Siemens' experiment spread. The Bretts heard about it. In January, 1850, they placed an order with the Gutta Percha Company of London for "twenty-five nautical miles of copper wire covered with great care in gutta-percha to half an inch in diameter."

The Bretts had taken the plunge. They were going to try to lay the first submarine cable in the world.

They knew it was still a gamble, for the von Siemens' cable hadn't really had a fair trial. Even if they got their cable laid, would an electrical impulse travel twenty-two miles under water? Very little was yet known about electricity. Not even the great Michael Faraday, or William Thomson, Professor of Natural Philosophy at Glasgow, really understood it.

Telegraphic transmission was a simple kind of electromagnetic operation based on the idea of making and breaking a circuit. Small batteries attached to the sending and receiving machines set up a flow of current. When the telegraphic key was pressed down, the circuit was closed. When the key was released, the circuit was open. A signaling code had been devised whereby short and long electrical impulses represented dots and dashes respectively. For this, tiny batteries and a very minimum of electricity were required.

For a long cable under water, the scientists thought that bigger batteries and a stronger electrical current should be used. Of course, this was exactly the wrong thing to do. The strong current, passing through the light wire, tended to destroy it. And a high voltage certainly was bad for the gutta-percha covering. But nobody knew that at the time.

All winter long the work on the cable went forward. The wire was drawn at the Bretts' own ropewalk. Then it was sent to the Gutta Percha Company to be covered.

Early in the summer the cable was ready. It was carted to the Thames, loaded in short lengths onto the small tug *Goliath* and floated down to Dover. At Dover the *Goliath* was tied up alongside the quay, and workmen began joining the cable into one length.

So many people gathered to watch that the cable men had a hard time getting on with the job. When nobody was looking the spectators snipped off little pieces of cable for souvenirs. They made slits in the gutta-percha to look at the shining wire inside.

"It's a crazy scheme," said one man. "That line couldn't be pulled twenty-five yards on land, let alone pretty near that number of miles at the bottom of the Channel."

Many others agreed that the whole idea was a big joke.

Somehow or other, the twenty-two-mile cable was pieced together. Then it was wound onto a large iron spool on the deck of the *Goliath* between her paddle wheels.

A length of cable was carried to shore, and one end was fastened to a box car in Dover Station. The rest was run across the road along Admiralty Pier and out into the sea where it dangled in the water.

A telegraph transmitter was set up and attached to the piece of cable connected to the box car. This bulky transmitter was geared to print letters instead of the much simpler dots and dashes of the Morse code.

Everything was ready—except the weather. The Bretts wanted a good day to cross the Channel.

The morning of August 28, 1850, dawned bright and sunny. There was no wind, the water was fairly smooth, and the day was so clear that the Bretts could see all the way across the Channel to the cliffs on the French side.

Jacob Brett boarded the *Goliath*. With him were a few old cronies whom he had invited for the ride.

John Brett wasn't going along. He was staying in Dover to send the first telegram, once the cable was laid.

At ten o'clock, with the twenty-two miles of cable behind her funnel, the little tug pulled out a short distance and then stood offshore in deep water.

Close by lay Her Majesty's surveying paddle ship *Widgeon*. The *Widgeon* had been sent to Dover by the British Admiralty to escort the *Goliath* across the Channel.

A crowd collected on the dock. They cheered as a small boat put out, carrying the end of the cable length which had been attached to the transmitter on shore. In a few minutes it was spliced to the twenty-two-mile length of cable on the *Goliath*.

Whistles tooted. Up came the anchor. Off went the *Goliath* toward the French coast. The *Widgeon* put about and got out in front, like a policeman, to warn Channel craft to keep clear.

At about four miles an hour, slowly and steadily paying out cable over her taffrail, the *Goliath* steamed toward the opposite shore. Pieces of cotton waste and wooden laths had been placed between the layers of cable. They flew out in all directions as the line uncoiled. Flat pieces of lead had been attached to the cable at every sixteenth of a knot to act as sinkers. They came loose, struck the ship, and rebounded.

Jacob Brett and his friends dodged around the deck in terror of their lives. They got in everybody's way. They bumped into the men who were working, and they tripped over the cable. Why it didn't break, nobody knew.

When the *Goliath* was halfway across, the London *Times* put out an extra edition. "Electro-Magnetic telegraph in Mid-Channel," the story read. "The project of sinking submarinely the lightning has begun."

The hours passed. Just before sundown, the *Goliath* dropped anchor off the white cliffs of Cape Gris Nez on the coast of France. The cable was attached to a receiver.

All day, John Brett on the English side had been watching the operation through a telescope. When he saw the tug stop, he put down his glasses. He waited till he judged the receivers were working and then he began sending his message:

Pieces of wooden lath flew in all directions.

"To the Honorable Louis Napoleon Bonaparte, President of France."

On the French side, the receiver key began to move. Everybody crowded around. The key clicked steadily for six minutes, then stopped.

Jacob Brett tore off the paper and looked. The letters were jumbled!

What had happened?

Nobody could figure it out.

The cable had been safely laid at the bottom of the Channel. The electric current was coming through properly. But what could have happened to the printing machine? The letters were completely scrambled. The message simply didn't make sense.

To Jacob Brett, as he held the printed tape in his hand, the garbled letters spelled just one word—F-A-I-L-U-R-E.

There was nothing to do but go back home and try again.

In the summer of 1851, a year later, the Bretts laid another cable. This time the signals came through clear and in order. The first readable undersea telegram in the world was at last delivered to the President of France.

3

The Telegraph Plateau

Today professional frogmen dive several hundred feet under water to explore sunken ships and salvage lost cargoes. They dig up samples of the ocean floor, take pictures under water, and test the currents with special instruments. In the deeper parts of the ocean, where divers can't go as yet, scientists are using modern techniques to help them solve the mysteries of the bottom.

At the time the cable was being laid between England and France, and Cyrus Field was dreaming about the Atlantic submarine cable, almost nothing was known about the ocean depths. Nobody had ever been down there and come back alive. There were some people who actually thought that in many places the ocean had no bottom.

About this time, a man named Matthew Fontaine Maury set out methodically to plumb the secrets of the ocean. Lieutenant Maury was a naval officer turned scientist. After an accident made him unfit for sea duty, he went to Washington to take charge of the Navy Department's Depot of Charts and Instruments. Historians sometimes call him the "Father of Oceanography."

Maury wanted to find out the exact depth of the seas. He knew from his own experience that all sea captains took "soundings." They had been doing it ever since Phoenician times. And they always noted their findings on the ship's log.

The simplest and oldest way of taking a sounding is to attach a sinker to a long string, swing it around like a lasso, and throw the sinker overboard. The line runs out. When the sinker hits bottom, the line stops running. The depth of the water can be determined by the amount of string which has run out.

The sounding lines used in Maury's day were more

The sinker was thrown overboard on a sounding line.

accurate than those used by the Phoenicians. The sinkers were big cannon balls shot out of cannon and the lines were of strong hemp rope. The rope was marked like a tape measure, with sea fathoms instead of inches. On the most modern ships the line was attached to a contraption called a Massey Indicator. The indicator measured the rope mechanically as the cannon ball sank to the bottom.

Maury made contact with sea captains all over the world and asked them to send him the records of their soundings. He collected thousands of reports from hundreds of captains. Then he studied the figures for a long time, comparing them with each other and marking the results on maps. This was the first time in history that anyone had charted the depths of each of the seven seas.

Next, Lieutenant Maury wanted to discover what went on in these ocean depths. Were there waves? Or strong currents? Or was the water still? What covered the bottom of the ocean? Was it sand, or silt, or earth? Were there rocks? Did anything grow down there? Were there fish or other sea animals?

During the summer of 1853 the United States brig *Dolphin* sailed on a voyage of "special service of research concerning the winds and currents of the sea." Maury ordered Lieutenant Berryman, her commander, "to make observations of that part of the ocean which merchantmen used as their great thoroughfare between Europe and the United States—Newfoundland to Ireland."

This was exactly the route which Cyrus Field had been thinking of for his submarine telegraph.

Mr. Field had spoken confidentially to several of his friends, and had their promise of backing if he should decide to go ahead. But he still wanted some scientific advice before he put time and effort and money into a small gutta-percha-covered wire and dropped it to the bottom of the Atlantic Ocean. So he wrote to Lieutenant Maury and asked his opinion of the venture.

As it happened, the Lieutenant had just been writing a letter to the Secretary of the Navy on this same subject, and he sent Mr. Field a copy. It was dated February 22, 1854, and was addressed to J. C. Dobbin, Secretary of the United States Navy.

On the first page of the report Lieutenant Maury told about the voyage of the *Dolphin*.

"Lieutenant Berryman . . . made a line of deep sea soundings from the shores of Newfoundland to those of Ireland," he wrote. "These soundings confirm the existence of a submarine continent between the two continents, a plateau which seems to have been placed there especially for the purpose of holding the wires of a submarine telegraph, and of keeping them out of harm's way. It is so deep that the wires once landed will remain forever beyond the reach of

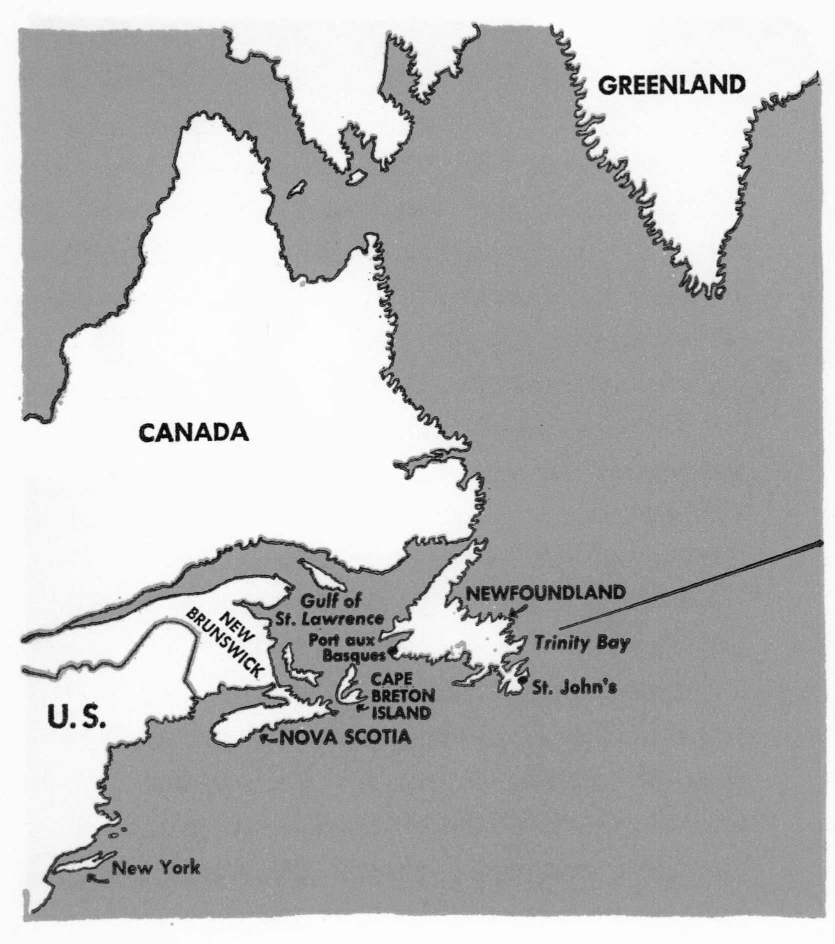

vessels' anchors, icebergs and drifts of any kind. It is so shallow that the wires may be readily lodged upon the bottom. The depth of this plateau is quite regular, gradually increasing from the shores of North Amer-

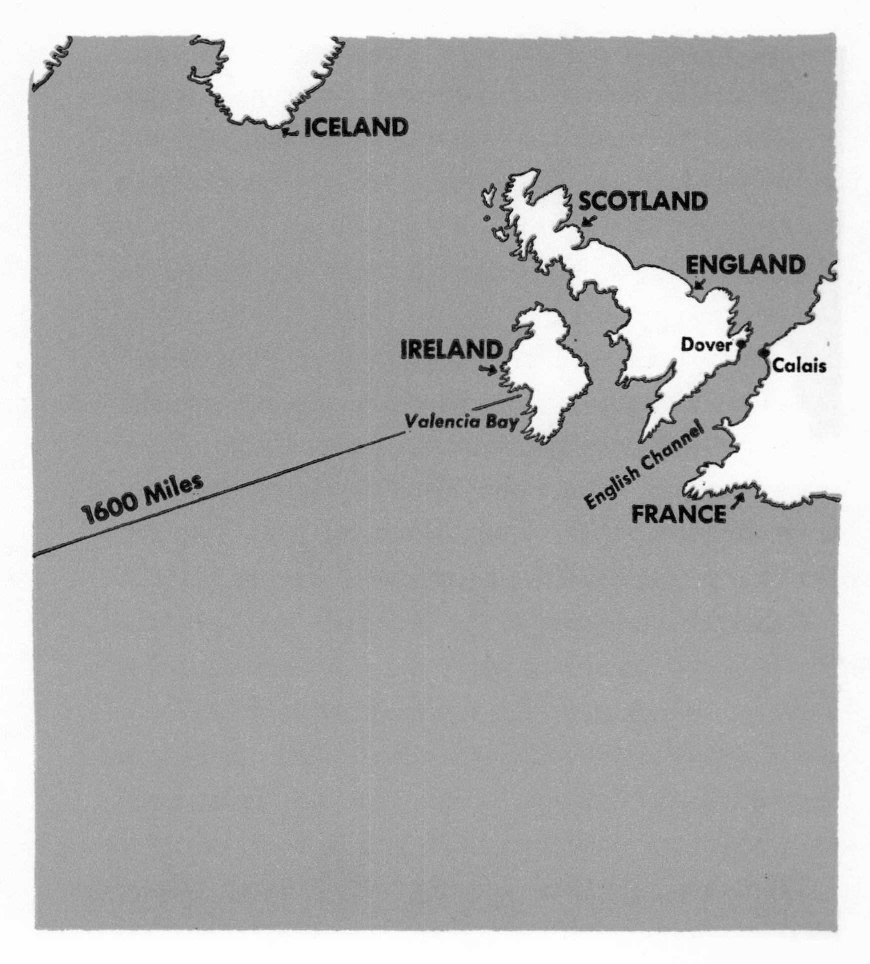

ica to a depth of 1,500 fathoms as you approach the other side.

"If there could be found *a time calm enough, the sea smooth enough, a wire long enough, a ship big enough* to lay a coil of wire 1,600 miles in length, insofar as *the bottom of the sea* is concerned, it can be done. I feel that the greatest difficulties will not be in the deep sea but after reaching the shallows at either end of the line."

Mr. Field breathed a sigh of relief. He turned to the next page.

"Using Brooke's Deep-Sea-Sounding Apparatus," he read, "Lieutenant Berryman brought up samples of the bottom from this plateau. I sent them to Professor Bailey of West Point, who examined them under a microscope. We were all surprised to find that these samples contain not a particle of sand or gravel."

Under the microscope the scientists had seen the tiny shells of billions of snails and mussels and other small fish which had once lived on the surface of the sea. When the little animals died, their shells had dropped to the bottom. There they lay, layer upon layer, still perfect after millions and millions of years.

"This would make us infer," Lieutenant Maury went on, "that these depths of the sea are not disturbed by either waves or currents. Down there, all is still.

"A telegraphic wire once laid there, there it would remain, as completely beyond the reach of accident as if it were buried in air-tight cases.

"Therefore, as far as the bottom of the deep sea between Newfoundland and Ireland is concerned, the practicability of a submarine cable across the Atlantic is proved."

4

A Visit from Professor Morse

Cyrus Field was glad to get Lieutenant Maury's report. But he also wanted very much to talk with Professor Samuel Finley Breese Morse before he made up his mind about the Atlantic telegraph project. He had been told that the Professor probably knew more about electric telegraphy than anybody else in the world. He wondered what the great inventor of the first practical electromagnetic telegraph would think were the chances of success.

Mr. Field wrote a letter to Professor Morse asking

for an appointment. Before the week was out the Professor came down to New York from Tarrytown to see Mr. Field.

Mr. Field was overcome by the honor. He took the great inventor into the library and invited him to sit on his own favorite chair, next to the fire. Then Mr. Field sat down in a straight chair opposite and plunged right into business.

"Do you believe, sir," he asked, "that the lightning can pass through the ocean? Do you believe that signals can be sent beneath the broad Atlantic's waters, and received two thousand miles away?"

The great inventor leaned back in his chair. His large brown eyes were dreamy, and a tremendous beard reached about halfway to his waist. He spoke slowly and softly.

"All great undertakings," he said at last, "carry in them an element of uncertainty. A man must be bold and steadfast to embark on such a project. He must be willing to take almost any risk before he can find the answer to his gamble.

"One of my earliest experiments," he went on, "was performed in the harbor of New York. As usual, I was hard up for money. I put an advertisement in the daily paper saying that for certain hours on a certain day I would accept messages from the public and transmit them by my electromagnetic telegraph printing machine from Castle Garden at the Battery to Governor's Island across the bay.

"The night before, with a friend, I stole down to the water's edge. We drove a stake into the ground and made fast one end of the line. Then we loaded the rest of the wire into a fisherman's dory. It was a fine moonlit night," Morse continued, "and we were able to keep clear of the boats lying in the harbor. While my friend rowed, I payed out the iron wire over the side. At last we reached Governor's Island and made fast the other end, attaching it to a receiving machine in a boathouse on the shore. Then we rowed back to the New York side and completed our job, setting up a sending machine in the big hall at Castle Garden.

"Early the next day a crowd gathered. People poured into the hall, ready to pay half a dollar to try out the new contraption. It looked as though all my troubles were over. I imagined that I was going to be able to collect enough money to go on with my experiments. We sent eight messages—four dollars' worth—almost enough to pay for our night's work. And then, suddenly, the line failed. There were hoots and catcalls. The few people whose messages had already been sent demanded their money back. At last the crowd left and I was alone. Everybody was now sure I was really a fraud.

"Later on," Morse explained, "we discovered that a fishing vessel in the harbor had caught its anchor in the line. When the crew brought it to the surface, the sailors had simply cut the line.

". . . I payed out the iron wire over the side."

"After that I stuck to the land where I could keep watch over my wires. I didn't make any more experiments in the water. But I had proved to my own satisfaction that messages *can* be sent under water."

By this time Mr. Field was actually sitting on the edge of his chair. He could scarcely wait to hear what Professor Morse was going to say next.

The great man put his hand inside his coat and took a paper from his vest pocket.

"Here is a copy of a letter which I wrote on August 10, 1843, nearly ten years ago," he said, as he unfolded the letter and smoothed it out on his knee. "It is addressed to the Honorable John Spencer, who was then the Secretary of the Treasury. It details the results of certain experiments which show the power of electricity to communicate at great distances. Here is the end of the letter:

" 'A telegraphic communication on the electromagnetic plan may with certainty be established across the Atlantic Ocean.'

"That was a startling thing to say in those days, but even then I was confident that the time would come when this project would be realized."

Professor Morse stood up.

"Mr. Field," he said, "I have never changed my mind. In the time that has elapsed since I sent that letter, telegraphs have been laid under smaller seas, proving that I was right in theory. But laying a transatlantic telegraph cable will be a costly venture. Even with your position in the community it will be difficult to get backing. You must ask yourself, before you start, do you have the spirit to carry it through to the end."

The Professor held out his hand to Mr. Field. "I can give no guarantee," he said, "but I am confident in my mind that once the cable is laid, the lightning *will* pass successfully under the ocean, connecting the New World with the Old."

After Dr. Morse had left, Cyrus Field went back into the library and put his hand on the globe in the corner. In all the world there was no one who could tell him with certainty what would be the outcome of this project. He was going to have to find out for himself.

He knew that come what might he would go ahead and try to lay the first transatlantic cable.

5

A Pleasure Excursion

On the morning of August 7, 1855, a horse-drawn cab pulled up at the entrance to Pier No. 4, North River, New York City.

John Mullaly of the New York *Herald* jumped out. He gave the cabbie twenty cents for his fare and a nickel tip, grabbed his carpetbag, and dodged in and out through the crowd of cabs, horses, ladies and gentlemen, and porters with trunks and portmanteaux that filled the street.

Alongside the pier lay the two-masted side-wheeler *James Adger,* steam up. At ten o'clock the *Adger* was sailing for Port-aux-Basques, Newfoundland. There she was scheduled to meet the cable ship *Sarah L. Bryant* out of London. The *Bryant* was carrying seventy-four miles of copper cable covered with gutta-percha which had been manufactured in England.

Between them, the *Adger* and the *Bryant* were going to try to lay that cable under the Gulf of St. Lawrence—the first lap of the Atlantic Submarine Electro-magnetic Project.

Jack Mullaly was going along on the *Adger* to write the story of the trip. It was a newspaperman's dream.

Mullaly pushed and elbowed his way along the pier. He'd never seen such a jam! It looked as though all New York was there. To make matters worse, piemen and pretzel sellers and souvenir vendors were calling their wares. Newsboys were darting in and out, offering dime novels, penny shockers, and the morning papers.

Mullaly shoved along to the gangplank and sprinted up to the deck. Hanging over the rail, watching the people on the pier, was the famous world-traveler, Bayard Taylor of the *Tribune,* along with Fitz-James O'Brien of the *Times* and three or four lesser reporters.

Jack joined the news hawks. He took out his pencil and pad and got ready to jot down the names of the notables as they came up the gangplank.

The first person he spotted was Mr. Peter Cooper, who had built the little Tom Thumb locomotive twenty years before and had given the money for the Cooper Union Labor College in New York City. Mr. Cooper was backing the Transatlantic Cable with a sizable sum of money, so he was good for a news item.

Right behind him were Professor S. F. B. Morse with Mrs. Morse. Mullaly added them to his list.

A stream of celebrities followed. Among them F. N. Gisborne passed unnoticed in the crowd. There were politicians and scientists and well-known preachers. There were businessmen, lawyers, and fashionable ladies and gentlemen whose names were always in the society columns. The New York, Newfoundland, and London Telegraph Company had invited them for the trip, and every single one of them seemed to have brought along some relations and hangers-on.

At two minutes to ten, the Field party came up the gangplank. In addition to Cyrus West Field the promoter, Dr. Henry M. Field the preacher, and

Cabs, horses, passengers and baggage crowded the pier.

David Dudley Field the lawyer, there were assorted male and female relatives. There were small girls in pantalets. There were dignified matrons wearing bonnets with veils and wide silk skirts. There were also gentlemen in top hats and cutaway coats.

The steam whistle on the *James Adger* let go a series of shrill hoots. There was a general confusion of good-bys and a great scramble of visitors leaving the ship.

It was sailing time!

"Let the hawser go there!" came a voice from the bridge.

The last rope was unfastened. The steam whistle gave out its last shriek. The *James Adger* began backing away, out into the river.

The people on the pier cheered. Ships that were docked as far north as Twenty-third Street and factories along both banks tooted. A salute of three guns was fired from the *Adger's* bow. A ship anchored off Hoboken let go an answering salute.

The *Adger* turned around and headed down the bay—past Brooklyn Heights on the left and Staten Island on the right, through The Narrows, and out into the open sea.

The crowd on the deck of the *Adger* thinned out. The newsmen hurried to their cabins to write up their stories. They were going to send them back from Port-aux-Basques by land telegraph. The scientists and a few businessmen gathered in the saloons to discuss the chances of success. But most of the passengers went below, laughing and chatting. They were in great spirits. They weren't thinking about the cable. They were looking forward to the trip as a pleasure excursion.

6

At Port-aux-Basques

"Our first night on the water was marked by a grand display of celestial pyrotechnics . . ." wrote Mr. Mullaly, who loved purple prose. "It appeared as if the powers of the air had determined to signalize our mission . . . in a peculiarly appropriate manner."

In plainer language, the pleasure excursion ran into a "rip-roaring" thunderstorm.

Professor Morse took advantage of the weather to set up an electric machine and reënact Franklin's experiment. But his audience was small, for there were more junketeers than serious-minded scientists on board.

Many of the passengers before long unwillingly sought shelter from the fury of the storm. The hardier ones, however, attended "a concert in the after cabin . . . in which all who had voice for music, and some who had not, joined."

When at last the concert had come to an end, "all retired for the night . . . the only sounds that broke the stillness . . . were the monotonous dash of the waves and the ceaseless din and clangor of the mighty machine."

The storm died down before morning. The sun came out, bright and clear, and the sea was calm. The ship's company reappeared topside.

Some of the party gathered to watch Professor Morse as he continued to make demonstrations of magnetic electricity. But most of the excursionists spent their days on deck enjoying themselves. The gentlemen played shuffleboard and quoits. The ladies stood by and applauded. At night there were concerts and dances and amateur theatricals in the main cabin, while the younger people went walking on the deck in the moonlight.

On August 12th the *James Adger* cast anchor in the

harbor of Port-aux-Basques. The *Sarah L. Bryant* was nowhere to be seen.

The excursionists were delighted. Their ship went on to St. John's, giving them a chance to go ashore and do some sightseeing in the largest town in Newfoundland. They attended a reception in Government House and spent several jolly days chatting with prominent local people. Some explored the surrounding wild country, with its woods and waterfalls and its mysterious "Spouting Rock." They also went to watch the natives spreading fish to dry on the "flakes" or frames along the shore, as their French ancestors had done in the same spot even before Columbus.

After several days the *Adger* returned to Port-aux-Basques and found that the *Sarah L. Bryant* had at last arrived. She was a much smaller vessel than the *Adger*. On board the *Bryant* was Samuel Canning, engineer for Glass, Elliot and Company of England. This firm had manufactured the cable, and Mr. Canning was to be in charge of all cable laying.

Though the weather had turned stormy, Mr. Canning ordered operations to begin. The first step was to set up a shelter on the beach for the shore end of the cable. One of the ships in the harbor, the *Victoria,* had brought along the frame and timber for a telegraph house. All of this material was loaded on an improvised raft and the raft was made fast to two small dories. Captain Sluyter of the *Victoria* and one of his men climbed aboard the raft. Sailors from the *Adger* took their places at the oars of the first dory.

Down into the second dory skylarked a crew of volunteer junketeers. Every one of them claimed to be a first-class oarsman. They dubbed themselves the "Submarine Telegraph Express" and shouted and laughed as they climbed into the little boat.

Mr. Canning, watching from the rail of the *Bryant,* shook his head. Captain Sluyter, balanced on the heaving raft, looked grim. He was in no mood for frolicking.

"Row ahead," he called. The dories shot through the heavy seas and into the mountain of breakers that crashed on the beach.

The breakers rolled over the dories, drenching the oarsmen and almost swamping the boats. Huge sections of the telegraph house were washed overboard. The raft split right down the middle. Captain Sluyter clung to one half and his helper to the other.

A crowd of native fishermen with their big black water dogs had gathered to watch. They were used to

The raft split right down the middle.

rescue work. At once they rushed out into the water, shoulder-deep, and waded to the boats. They seized the floating timbers and the helpless dories, and half pushed and half carried them to shore.

The dogs, too, plunged into the surf. They paddled around. Holding their heads high, they grabbed floating objects in their teeth and carried them to safety.

The volunteers, glad to be alive, slapped each other

on the back, hugged the dogs, and shook hands with their rescuers.

The sailors didn't waste any time. They went right to work setting up the frame telegraph house.

The next day two small boats from the *Adger* were loaded with cable, lashed together, and towed ashore by the natives. A log had been sunk through the floor of the telegraph house, and a hogshead set atop it. The cable was brought up, wound around the hogshead and moored. The shore end of the telegraph was ready.

Now for the Gulf of St. Lawrence!

7

Across the Gulf of St. Lawrence

The next morning the *Adger* and the *Bryant* were hidden from each other in a blanket of fog. There was nothing to do but lay to. The cable fleet couldn't put out to sea in such weather.

Captain Pousland of the *Bryant* and Mr. Canning chafed over the delay. But the members of the "Submarine Telegraph Express" were in high spirits. They hadn't had a chance the day before to inspect the telegraph shack. They decided to go ashore now and take a look.

Without telling the Captain, they sneaked away in a small boat. At once they were lost in the fog.

Hour after hour dragged by. Had the dory foundered on a rock? Had it drifted out to sea? Was the pleasure excursion turning into a disaster? Watchers hung over the rail, but they couldn't see a thing.

Just at sundown shouts were heard. Out of the fog the lost boat appeared alongside the *Adger*. The junketeers, frightened and bedraggled, climbed up the ladder to the deck. The Captain and Mr. Canning ordered them into the saloon and delivered a lecture.

There would be no more nonsense, they declared, and they threatened to set the junketeers on shore and leave them there until the serious object of the cable fleet had been accomplished.

Mr. Field and Professor Morse spoke up for the passengers and promised that there would be no more foolishness if they were allowed to stay on board.

The next morning the fog lifted, but stormy weather set in. Just the same, the fleet got ready to put out.

The shore end of the cable was spliced to the rest of the line coiled on the deck of the *Bryant*. Then, after repeated failures, a towing hawser from the *Adger* was made fast to the *Bryant*. Since the *Adger* was a steamship, she was going to tow the sailing vessel.

The paddle wheels on the *Adger* began to revolve. With the sailing vessel in tow, the steamship started for open water. But the troubles had only begun. The *Bryant's* anchor stuck and had to be cut before she could get under way. Then suddenly, out of control, she came bearing down on the *Adger*. In spite of everything, there was a collision, and for a few moments it looked as though the expedition was over before it had even begun. But by a miracle the damage was slight.

After a long delay, the fleet at last put out to sea. It was a sunny, fair morning and the prospects of success seemed assured. However, once they were outside the harbor, the *Adger* and the *Bryant* couldn't get their speeds synchronized. The tow line and the cable were constantly getting entangled.

The cable was wound around a drum made of wood and passed across the deck of the *Bryant* into the water over another drum at her stern. As it was payed out, men operating hand brakes stood by to watch for kinks or faults. When they saw any imperfection they applied the hand brakes and set up a shout. Their shouts were the signal for the *Adger* to reverse her engines and stop while repairs were made. The bad piece of cable was cut out and a new piece spliced to the ends. Then the fleet could proceed again.

An operation like this, with all the stopping and starting, needed split-second timing. The steamers of those days were not geared for such ticklish work, particularly when they had a sailing vessel in tow. The whole performance became a nightmare.

Before forty miles of line had been laid, nearly everybody had decided that the only thing to do was to cut the cable and abandon the whole project. However, the decision was up to Mr. Canning—and Mr. Canning wouldn't give up. There was too much at stake.

Captain Pousland pointed out that he had something at stake, too. He was responsible for the lives of the people on board. Most of them were sick. And all of them were frightened.

"What did they come for?" asked Mr. Canning, shrugging his shoulders. "This is a place for serious people. I'll leave it to Mr. Field."

But Mr. Field refused to give the word to turn back.

In the late afternoon a twenty-five-mile-an-hour wind came up. It was a real gale. The two vessels linked together with a hawser were blown this way

"Do you need help?" the Commander shouted.

and that. They were in danger of tearing each other to pieces. And the cable trailing behind the *Bryant* was an added hazard.

During the height of the gale the British war steamer *Argus* crossed their course. Sighting the ships floundering in the heavy seas, she hove to and came within hailing distance.

"Do you need help?" shouted her commander, Captain Purvis, through a big megaphone. Captain Sluyter leaned over the rail of the bridge of the *Victoria* and shouted back. But the wind was in the wrong direction and no matter how loud he yelled he couldn't make the people on the *Argus* hear him. The weather was too bad to put out a boat. And the night was too dark for signaling.

All night the *Argus* stood by. All night Captain Purvis stood on the bridge, expecting every moment to see the cable fleet break up in the pounding sea.

By morning the wind had died down and the sun was shining. A man standing on the paddle box of the *Argus* held up a blackboard on which was written in white letters: *CAN WE RENDER YOU ANY ASSISTANCE?*

At first there was no response. A second board was hoisted on the *Argus: ANSWER YES OR NO.*

Then at last the *Adger* answered. On her smokestack in white chalk was written the single word: *NO*.

It was too late for anyone to help. The ships and their passengers were safe. But during the night, Mr. Canning, hard-pressed, had given the grim order to cut the cable.

Forty miles of the precious line lay at the bottom of the Gulf of St. Lawrence.

8

Gold Dollars and Pounds Sterling

Early in the summer of 1856, a new cable fleet set out for Newfoundland to make another try at laying a line under the Gulf of St. Lawrence. It was strictly a business trip. There wasn't any fanfare, there weren't any gay troublesome junketeers aboard, there weren't any newspapermen. Even Mr. Field didn't go along. He was too busy with the money end of the venture.

The money had been put up by the three Field brothers, Professor Morse and five other American businessmen. The two Bretts had been able to get the cable manufactured on speculation. The nine Americans and John Brett were the owners of the company, as well as the board of directors. Fifty thousand dollars had gone to Mr. Gisborne to pay his debts. He was now out of the company.

It was costing about one million dollars to run the first lap of cable from Newfoundland to New York. After the cable fleet left for Newfoundland, the directors held a meeting. They did a little arithmetic. They figured that it would take perhaps a couple of million dollars more to get the cable clear across the ocean.

They couldn't raise that much among themselves. But after all, the submarine cable was an international affair. Why not try to raise some of the money on the other side of the Atlantic?

So Cyrus Field boarded the *Baltic,* a Cunard ship bound for Southampton, England. Mr. Brett was waiting for him there. Right away the two of them started trying to organize a new company, to be called the Atlantic Telegraph Company.

The English were leading the world in inventions. An Englishman had built the first practical stationary steam engine. And that had been followed by a regular epidemic of new developments—locomotives that went twenty miles an hour, railroads and factories, iron bridges and steamships.

The new British industrialists had the money and the influence to put over the new Atlantic Telegraph Company. John Brett was one of them, and he took Mr. Field around to meet many others. They visited everybody who had something to do with submarine telegraphy. There were the men who had laid the cable from Sardinia to Italy and from Italy to Corsica. There were also men who were stringing wires under the Mediterranean from Africa to France and others who were working to join Ireland to England by a line under the Irish Sea. Each of them had suggestions. Many were even willing to gamble with some of their money.

Charles Bright, engineer for the Magnetic Telegraph Company, was one of the first to join the enterprise. He had helped lay the first cable between England and Ireland, and he was a British national hero. During the Crimean War he had laid a secret line under the Black Sea from Varna to Balaklava.

Brett also took Field to see Robert Stephenson. As a young man Stephenson had helped his father build the Comet, the first practical steam locomotive in the world. Now Robert was a big railroad mogul. He listened to Field's story and promised to go into the venture.

The two men also visited Daniel Gooch, who was a colorful figure in England at the time. He had been a locomotive engineer and had driven the train when Queen Victoria made her first trip by rail. Now he was one of the biggest railway magnates in England. He had shipbuilding interests, too.

"I'll give you my blessing," said Gooch, "but I can't take on anything new. I'm up to my neck building the *Great Eastern*. I'm committed with all my money to Brunel."

Brunel! He was the man whom Cyrus Field most wanted to talk to.

Isambard Kingdom Brunel had built railway stations and railroads in England, in Italy, in France, and even in far-off India. He had bridged the unbridgeable Firth of Forth in the west of Scotland with the longest iron span in the world. He had helped his father dig the undiggable tunnel under the Thames River. He had invented the tunnel shield that is still used today for underwater subways.

Though Mr. Brunel had big ideas, he was less than five feet tall. People called him the "Little Giant."

Everybody knew about the *Great Eastern,* Brunel's current project. She was a real fairy-tale boat. Her paddle wheels were as high as a two-story house. She could carry 12,000 passengers, and she needed a crew as big as the population of a town. She was scheduled for the India trade, and she was so fast that she would clip a whole week off the running time from London around the Cape of Good Hope to Bombay.

Brunel spent most of his time supervising every bit of work on the big ship. But he kept dashing off to other parts of the world to promote his many ventures and to get money for his "beautiful leviathan," as he called the *Great Eastern.*

No wonder Mr. Field couldn't catch up with him!

One day Cyrus Field went down to the west coast of England to take a look at the Irish Sea cable. Toward evening, at a little town called Milford Haven, he caught a train for London. He climbed into a railway carriage and settled down in the corner.

There were three other men in the compartment. Two of them were deep in talk. The third man was hunched up on the seat opposite Mr. Field reading a newspaper. Mr. Field could see only the top of his stove-pipe hat.

Suddenly the stranger slammed down his newspaper and glared around him. Mr. Field took one look. He couldn't believe his luck. Here he was locked up in a railway compartment with Isambard Kingdom Brunel!

He didn't waste a moment. Leaning forward, he asked:

"Mr. Isambard Kingdom Brunel? . . ."

Brunel gave him a sour look.

"My name is Cyrus Field," Mr. Field went on quickly. "I'm here in England in the interests of . . ."

The Little Giant held up his hand. "Not another

word," he interrupted. "I know who you are and I've been wanting to meet you, but I haven't been able to catch up with you." He pulled out a big watch and opened it.

"We have just four hours," he said. "Don't waste a moment of it. Get down to business. Tell me right away about that transatlantic magnetic telegraph of yours. How are things going for you?"

"The first thousand miles are nearly completed," Mr. Field began. "Our expedition last year failed, you know. But we learned a lot and we hear nothing but good reports of the fleet that is laying the last miles across the Gulf of St. Lawrence. By early fall, we will certainly be able to send a message without interference from New York to Newfoundland. This is more than a thousand miles."

"Good, good." Mr. Brunel nodded approval.

"Now, having reached the farthest point of the American coast, we stand upon the cliffs of Newfoundland, looking off across the wide sea toward England."

"Yes, yes," said Mr. Brunel. "I understand all that. To put it bluntly, you are now up against the toughest part of your job. Spanning the Atlantic. This is the big gamble. It'll take money—a lot of it. And then there are all the scientific questions—the electricity, the cable, the machines to lay the cable. How are you getting along with that?"

"That's why we came to England," Field answered. "I'm trying to get backers for an English telegraph company to put up the money to match our American dollars. Professor Samuel Morse is here with me——"

"Professor Morse!" interrupted Brunel. "There's a man I want to know."

"I'll be glad to arrange it," said Field, throwing away his usual business caution. "He's been hoping to meet you ever since we got here."

"Name your own time," said Brunel. "I'll be there. I want you to come with me to the Isle of Dogs in the Thames and see my *Great Eastern* where she lies in the ways. She's a beauty. She'd be a perfect ship to lay a cable."

"Could we get her?" asked Field, leaning forward anxiously.

"No chance." The Little Giant laughed. "Too costly. She's got to pay her way by carrying passengers between England and India. Too bad, too bad."

"From what I understand," said Mr. Field, "the *Great Eastern* would solve many of our worries. We have to transport 3,000 miles of cable, and that's a big load for a ship."

"My beauty could carry every inch of it," said Brunel, shaking his head. "You could stow it in her hold and have room to spare. There's not another ship afloat that could do that. Too bad."

"What we've decided to do," said Mr. Field, "is to divide the cable in two, put half on one ship and half on another. We'll send the two vessels out to the middle of the Atlantic to a rendezvous; they'll splice the cable there and proceed in opposite directions, one toward the New World and one toward the Old."

"Mmmm," said Brunel. "Even so, you'll have to get good, big, steady ships."

"We're working on making a lighter cable. Professor Morse is conferring with John Brett on that very subject." Field took four inches of cable out of his pocket and handed it to Brunel. "This is the type that Professor Morse prefers at the moment," he said.

Brunel wore a magnifying glass around his neck on a ribbon. He screwed the glass into his right eye and peered at the sample, turning it round and round. "Mmmm," he said. "The usual thing—the core of twisted copper wire covered with what I take to be waterproof gutta-percha. Good. Excellent. Insist that the copper wire be the purest that you can get. That ensures a steady flow of the electricity. Don't be satisfied with anything but the best."

Mr. Field made a note of this.

"But I don't like the coating." Mr. Brunel was in the habit of speaking his mind. "The armor's too stiff and too heavy—no give." He tried to work it back and forth in his stubby-fingered hands, testing it and trying to bend it this way and that. "Let's see," he said. "What would make it more flexible?"

His face lighted up. "Why not make the casing of a twisted iron wire, coiled around the inner wire like a spring? Then dip the whole thing in gutta-percha. I've seen the machines they have in these manufactories. They can make the cable come out like a thick piece of macaroni, with the electric wire inside. There'll be plenty of 'give' to that. You tell John Brett for me that that's the way to do it."

Mr. Field and Mr. Brunel had forgotten all about their traveling companions. Now one of the gentlemen leaned forward.

"Allow me to introduce myself," he said. "My

name is Glass. And this," he added, nodding toward his friend, "is Mr. Elliot. We are the firm of Glass and Elliot . . ."

"Glass and Elliot!" Mr. Field exclaimed. "Imagine your being here at this time. Mr. Brunel, these are the two gentlemen who helped manufacture the casing for the St. Lawrence project."

"For that, and for many other submarine telegraphs," said Mr. Glass.

"What a fortunate meeting," said Mr. Field.

"From our experience," said Mr. Glass, "we have learned that Mr. Brunel is absolutely right about the quality of the copper wire. We were constantly plagued during the laying of the cable under the Channel by the impurities in the transmitting wires supplied for our casings. This prevented the electricity from flowing freely. But they've been able to improve this in later cables."

"And what about my casing?" said Mr. Brunel. "That's a good, practical idea, isn't it?"

"As usually happens," said Mr. Glass, bowing, "Mr. Brunel has come up with a sound suggestion. If you will permit us we will make some trial samples at once, using the method you describe, and make tests. Perhaps you could manage to be present."

"Get Faraday. Get Thomson," said Mr. Brunel, waving his hand. "They know more about these scientific things than I do. I'm just a plain mechanic."

Mr. Glass smiled. He knew better.

"I got my engineering in America," said Brunel. "Americans like Mr. Field and me, we're practical men. But I'll come down and look at it anyway, just for the fun of it."

By the time the train reached London, Mr. Brunel had promised to throw his weight behind the cable company.

After this the money began to roll in. Scientists and businessmen were eager to invest when they heard that Brunel had given the venture his okay. Lords and ladies subscribed in flocks. Mr. Field and Mr. Brett soon found they had plenty of English pounds to match their American dollars. As quickly as possible, they took out the papers necessary for incorporation and sent the stock to the shareholders.

9

Cutting Red Tape

But even with all the money subscribed the Atlantic submarine telegraph project couldn't be launched unless both the English and the American governments would lend a hand.

Tying two big countries together with a thread of wire was an international affair. It meant treaties, the passing of laws, the chartering of ships, and perhaps even government subsidies. There was a lot of red tape to be cut.

Mr. Field wanted to start at once to present his

idea to Parliament. But Mr. Brett warned him against going ahead too fast.

"You have to be careful about using too much Yankee push on us careful English," he said. "Our House of Commons would never go along with a big thing like this on the word of even such a great man as Professor Samuel Morse. We'll have to think up some way of proving that an electromagnetic telegraph message *can* be sent 2,000 miles under water."

"The only way to prove that," said Mr. Field, "is to do it. We can't prove that we can send a message until the cable is laid. It's like a dog chasing his tail."

Mr. Brett smiled. He was used to Mr. Field's American eagerness.

"Charlie Bright and Dr. Whitehouse have got something figured out," he said. "I think it'll work. It'll take a little while to prepare. When we're ready we'll call in you and Professor Morse."

Four weeks later Brett notified Field that everything was ready for the experiment. Mr. Field and Professor Morse were instructed to come at midnight to the office of the Magnetic Telegraph Company in Old Broad Street, London. They were not to tell a soul about it.

They found Mr. Brett, Mr. Bright and Dr. Whitehouse waiting by the light of a single kerosene lamp like a bunch of conspirators. Talking in whispers, Brett took them into the cellar. A big iron vat was standing in the middle of the floor. In it were coiled 2,000 miles of insulated copper wire, spliced together and covered with water. To one end of the cable they had attached a telegraph sending machine and to the other end a receiving set.

While the conspirators looked on, Professor Morse sat down at the sending machine; Bright took the receiver. Professor Morse pressed down the transmission key. The impulse traveled all along the wire and came out good and strong at Bright's end.

Now Professor Morse began tapping out a message. The receiver responded merrily. The paper tape revolved. The pencil jumped up and down. There in plain sight was a whole readable telegram of dots and dashes.

Just to prove that it was no accident, Dr. Whitehouse took the key. Then Brett. The messages all came through.

Brett had proved Professor Morse's theory. An electric current *could* travel through 2,000 miles of wire under water and print a message at the other end. Mr. Field didn't have to wait any longer. He had his proof to present officially. He wrote a letter to the Earl of Clarendon, Lord Commissioner of Her Majesty's Treasure. In it he described the Atlantic cable project and asked "for the aid which was due to what concerned the honor and interest of England."

At the same time he wrote a second letter, this one to the British Admiralty. He described Lieutenant Maury's theory and told how Lieutenant Berryman had found the telegraph plateau. He asked that the British government make its own survey of the route, for he knew by this time that the English would never accept the American findings without their own verification. Finally, he requested that the Admiralty assign ships to help lay the cable.

Lord Clarendon was the first to answer. He invited Mr. Field and Professor Morse to come to the Foreign Office for a talk.

The meeting was a short one. Mr. Field rather soft-pedaled the difficulties that might lie ahead. He gave a glowing account of the experiment that had been made in the cellar at Old Broad Street. He built up the possibilities of success and "the great benefits to be gained by both England and America through swift communication."

"But suppose you don't succeed," said Lord Clarendon. "Suppose you make the attempt and fail—your cable is lost in the sea. Then what will you do?"

"Charge it to profit and loss and go to work and lay another," Mr. Field answered quickly.

"That is a truly American reply," Lord Clarendon said, laughing, "and a very good one."

Then he added very seriously: "But you're right. Nothing is gained without a gamble. This is a truly great international work."

He stood up. "Put your request in writing," he said. "Without committing the government, I think I may say that you may hope that Britain will do all that might justly be expected in aid of the completion of the submarine telegraph."

He was as good as his word. Within a short time, the cable promoters were handed a contract.

The contract promised £350,000—about $1,750,000—and a ship to take soundings and more ships to lay down the cable. In return, the company was to carry the government messages for twenty-five years "or for as long a time as it would take to repay at regular message rates the money invested."

Furthermore, the contract specified, "the British Government shall have a priority in the conveyance of their messages over all others, subject to the ex-

Mr. Brett led them down into the cellar.

ception only of the Government of the United States in the event of their entering into an arrangement with the telegraph company similar . . . to that of the British Government, in which case the messages of the two governments shall have priority in the order in which they arrive at the station."

Mr. Field and Mr. Brett were a step nearer their goal. They had won the promise of the British government to back the submarine cable project on its own, if necessary. Or the British stood ready to go into partnership with the United States, if and when America should decide to enter into the great gamble.

Even before the contract was signed, the Admiralty ordered the British vessel *Cyclops* on a research voyage from Ireland to Newfoundland to make its own check on Lieutenant Maury's reports of the "telegraph plateau."

Since these reports were based on the logs of two voyages already made by Lieutenant Berryman for the United States Navy, Mr. Field was a little annoyed. He thought the English were being more careful than usual. But Mr. Brett pointed out that this was a political move. The politicians—whether

English or American—had to have something of their own to show to the voters.

"Now that you've got the English telegraph company charter in your hand, and the British government contract in your pocket," said Mr. Brett, "it's a good time for you to go back home and tackle your own politicos."

In a few days Mr. Field and Professor Morse sailed for America to tackle the job of cutting red tape on that side of the water.

10

Congress Takes a Vote

Getting aid from the government of the United States was quite a different thing from getting government aid in England. The American Constitution did not provide for a Lord of the Treasury like the British Lord Clarendon, who could practically on his own deliver a contract.

In America a bill had to be brought up, debated and voted on in both Houses of Congress. Then it must be signed by the President before it became law.

There were only thirty-one states in the Union, but the country was already divided into sections—North, South and West. Each section had definite interests. However, there weren't as yet enough Western representatives to carry much weight. So the real split was between the North and the South.

A large number of the Northern senators represented shipowners, factory-owners, mine-owners, ironmasters and businessmen, as well as the thousands of people who worked in these trades. These people needed a foreign market for the things they manufactured.

The Southern senators represented the owners of plantations, gentlemen farmers who were interested principally in raising and selling cotton. Since a good part of this cotton was sold in the United States, mostly in the North, the Southerners didn't care very much about international trade. They were not likely to be interested in such a project as a transatlantic cable.

But Mr. Field believed that the Atlantic submarine cable was a good thing for the whole United States and he hoped to get the Senate solidly behind it. He sent a letter to President Franklin Pierce, asking him to start the ball rolling.

President Pierce called in Senator William B. Seward of New York and asked him to submit a bill to the Senate.

Senator Seward understood politics. He knew some senators would be against the project just because the idea had originated in New York City. He'd have to have some powerful Southern senators on his side if he wanted to win. So he went to work behind the scenes.

Senator Thomas Rusk of Texas and Senator Judah P. Benjamin of Louisiana promised to help. They went around among the other senators from below the Mason-Dixon line and built up strong support for a showdown on the Senate floor.

When he was sure of his backers, Senator Seward brought in the bill. It came up for debate.

Senator Rusk took the floor at once. He spoke for almost two hours. He brought up all the good points of an Atlantic submarine cable. He pointed out that the cable would be of great benefit to America. The United States ought to be a partner in its control, he stated.

The fat was in the fire! The argument started and grew hotter and hotter. The strongest opposition came from the Southern senators. Mr. Hunter of Virginia pointed out that both ends of the telegraph were within British domain.

"What security are we to have that in time of war we, as well as the British government, shall have the use of the telegraph?"

Senator Jones of Tennessee delivered a ranting oration against any partnership at all with England.

"England is our traditional enemy," he said in conclusion. "Let the British do it. I do not want to have anything to do with England or with Englishmen." And he sat down, bursting with patriotism.

Mr. Benjamin of Louisiana spoke for the bill:

"Let us not always be thinking of war; let us be using means to preserve peace. Among the things which will bind us together in peace, this telegraphic wire will be one of the most potent. These cords of iron will hold us in the bonds of peace."

Senator Bayard, of the border state of Delaware, added his support. "Times have changed," he said. "A war with England is not in the offing. We are friends now, bound together by mutual interests of commerce and trade.

"I look upon this telegraph proposition as a business venture. I believe our government will get more service for the amount of money put into it than by any other contract we have ever made for the transmission of intelligence."

The opposition took another tack. Senators delivered long, flowery speeches about the sanctity of the American Constitution. Spending money on this cable thing was unconstitutional!

"It's just as constitutional," Senator Bayard argued, "to put money into a submarine cable for the transmission of telegrams, as is the employment of a stagecoach or a steam car or a ship to transport the mails. Anything that has to do with communications can properly come under the Post Office Department."

When Senator Bayard sat down, Senator Rusk got up again. This would be a fine chance to give the Navy something to do, he declared.

"Our ships are idle," he said. "They have coal on board and they are full of armament. I think it is better to send them out on this errand than to keep them rotting in the Navy Yards with the officers frolicking on the shore."

Senator Seward summed up all the arguments. He took a long time to do it. He went all the way back to Benjamin Franklin, "the great and wise American who had discovered that lightning could be used as an agent for the needs of human society."

The argument grew hotter and hotter.

He reviewed the history of Professor Morse. "It was this man, a citizen of the United States, who first indicated to the government the means by which lightning could be made to write.

"This great invention," Senator Seward thundered, "is now to be brought by other Americans into its wider and broader use—the use by the general society of nations—the use of the society of mankind itself. The benefits are great, far beyond what we can now predict. They are not merely benefits to the government of our fair country! They are benefits to the citizens and the subjects of all nations and of all states! Let this august body make haste to confer these benefits for the good of humanity!"

Senator Seward sat down.

"Question! Question!" came voices from all parts of the Senate Chamber. There was a show of hands.

The decision was close! When the hands were counted the "ayes" won by a single vote.

The bill then went to the House of Representatives. Here it met with more oratory, more objections and more politics. But it passed!

President Franklin Pierce signed the bill.

The United States became a partner in the gamble of the Atlantic submarine cable.

11

Cheers, Peers and Parties

On the fourteenth of May, 1857, the American naval vessel *Niagara* dropped anchor off Gravesend, a small port in the Thames about twenty-five miles below London. The *Niagara* was the ship the United States government had picked to help lay the Atlantic submarine telegraph.

The plan adopted for the cable-laying was the one Mr. Field had outlined to Mr. Brunel. The *Niagara* was to pick up one half of the cable, proceed to Valencia Bay in Ireland, moor one end there and then sail west across the Atlantic, paying out the line until it was used up. There in mid-ocean the *Agamemnon,* a British ship loaded with the rest of the cable, would rendezvous with her. The two cable halves would be spliced, and the *Agamemnon* would then carry on the cable-laying, finishing the job in Newfoundland.

A United States ship would thus lay the European half of the telegraph; an English ship, the American half. It would be a real international partnership.

The *Niagara* was the largest steam frigate in the world, heavier than the biggest battleship in the English Navy. She was a three-masted square-rigger, for, like most steamers of her day, she carried sails in case the steam didn't work. She had a newfangled screw propeller instead of paddle wheels, and could easily make ten or twelve miles an hour.

The *Niagara* was a fine sight as she came up the Thames, sails spread and smoke belching from her funnel. As the American congressmen had predicted, she was something to make the British sit up and take notice.

Under the command of Captain William L. Hudson, the *Niagara* had put out from the Brooklyn Navy Yard less than fourteen days before. Everything had been very hush-hush and top-secret. The Navy had

The Niagara *was a fine sight steaming up the Thames.*

allowed no junketeers on this trip. In addition to the officers and the crew, there were only two observers for the Russian Navy and Professor Morse and his "secretary."

The "secretary" was John Mullaly of the New York *Herald,* who had been chosen official historian of the enterprise. This trip would assure him of a scoop.

The *Niagara* was the first of the cable fleet to show up at Gravesend. The *Susquehanna,* her consort ship, had left the Brooklyn Navy Yard on the same day as the big frigate. But she was only halfway across the Atlantic. The British *Agamemnon* and her consort, *Leopard,* were still on overseas duty for the Admiralty.

The British press and the public went wild when the news got out of the arrival of the *Niagara.* It was the first time that an American naval ship had ever come to England on a visit of friendship.

Captain Hudson had been ordered to "gain the good will of the English people." He declared open house. Parties came down from London to sightsee. There were families of excursionists with noisy boys and girls and even infants in arms. Fashionable ladies, gentlemen in top hats and a half dozen peers and peeresses made the trip.

The Gravesend Harbor swarmed with little boats shuttling back and forth, loaded to the gunwales with the curious. The *Niagara's* own tenders and dinghies were put at the service of the visitors. Everybody agreed that "the Yankees were most civil." And everybody admired the ship.

"If they call this a frigate," said one tough old weather-beaten salt who came aboard, "I dunna what their *liners* be!"

At last the *Agamemnon* came steaming up the river. As she passed the *Niagara* her crew lined up on the decks. Some sailors climbed to the tops of the masts and out onto the crossbeams.

"Three thundering cheers burst from her decks and shrouds," reported Mullaly. "Our men answered with one long 'Hurrah.' "

The crowd on the shore and in the harbor cheered and waved. "The noise was like a whirlwind."

The *Agamemnon* wasn't as big as the *Niagara,* but she had a long, proud record. She was a veteran of the Crimean War, had been at the siege of Sebastopol and had been peppered by the Russian shore batteries. She was a great favorite with the English people.

The *Agamemnon* had barely dropped her hook when the American *Susquehanna* arrived. The *Susquehanna* was the largest paddle-wheel ship afloat. Only the *Great Eastern* was larger, but she was not yet out of the ways.

When the *Leopard* came in, the cable fleet was ready. It was really an impressive sight.

At last the parties were over. The time had come for loading the cable.

12

Valencia Bay

Off the west of Ireland, in County Kerry, a narrow, rocky island sticks out into the ocean from the coast. Beyond this little island there is a chain of rocks, and then only the open sea. This thin, bony finger of land, called Valencia, points directly toward the American continent, across the mainstream of the North Atlantic.

In 1857 there were not more than two thousand people living on the whole island. Like their ancestors, they were fine seamen and great fishermen. Fish was still their staple food. The only village on the island was Knightstown. It was just a handful of rough stone buildings around a bare marketplace.

In the very center of Valencia, high up on a mountain, stood the stone fortress-castle of Lord Hillsborough, the Knight of Kerry. The Knight owned the whole island and everything on it. The work of the people belonged to him, and the better part of everything they caught, raised or mined went to him.

Lord Hillsborough spent most of his time in Cork or Dublin or in London. He didn't like living at the castle. Valencia was such an out-of-the-way place—so lonely, so cut off from the world!

Then Valencia was selected as the location for the European end of the Atlantic submarine cable, and everything changed.

Hundreds of laborers and linesmen and telegraph operators came over from England. They built a shack on the edge of the bay. They set up a sending machine and electric batteries in the shack. They ran wires from the shack to the mainland. These wires ran all the way across Ireland to the east coast, and were hooked up to the cables which crossed under the Irish Sea to Liverpool.

Messages were flashed direct from Valencia to London. Valencia was suddenly on the front pages of the big city newspapers all over the world. It wasn't cut off any longer.

Now came the great news from London that the cable fleet was on its way to Valencia Bay.

The islanders quit work. They packed up their children and their goats and their chickens and their scraggly pigs and trekked toward the bay. There they set up camp on the bluffs around the harbor and waited.

It was just like a fair. Strolling players and dancing bears entertained the children. Men ran races and played bowls. Every night fiddlers scraped out jigs, and men, women and children danced around the campfires.

For a whole week the fun went on.

Early on the morning of August 4th, word went around that some ships were coming into the harbor. The campers crowded to the edge of the bluff. On the beach below they could see a fleet of small private boats making a landing.

The people cheered and cheered as Lord Hillsborough stepped ashore. Lord Morpeth, Lord Lieutenant of Ireland, followed and they cheered again.

Last came a large party of gentlemen led by Mr. Field, his telegraph associates and some newspaper men. The crowd didn't know who they were, but they cheered all the same.

The party had hurried up from Cork to meet the cable fleet. It was true! At last the cable fleet was really coming!

Morning slipped into afternoon, and afternoon into evening. The picnickers sat down and waited. The gentlemen walked about and fussed and fretted. The sun began to go down.

Suddenly a roar went up from the crowd. The *Niagara* swung around the point and into the harbor. Six more ships of the cable fleet were right on her heels.

There was the *Agamemnon* with the two consort ships, *Susquehanna* and *Leopard.* And behind them sailed Her Majesty's steamer *Cyclops,* just returned from her trip "in the interests of science." She had made the run to Newfoundland and back in good time. The soundings she had taken in both directions had checked with the earlier American ones of Lieutenant Berryman.

The *Cyclops* was a gallant three-master, smaller

than the *Agamemnon* but sharper and faster. She was to go ahead of the cable fleet and chart the course.

Following the *Cyclops* came the little steamers *Advice* and *Willing Mind*. They weren't seagoing craft. They had come to Valencia to do the job of carrying the shore end of the cable from the *Niagara* through the shallow waters of the bay to the beach.

The fleet hove to and dropped anchor well out in deep water. By this time it was night. Operations would have to wait until the sun came up again.

Mr. Field and the officials of the telegraph company put out from shore in rowboats. As members of the expedition, they were quartered aboard the ships.

Lord Morpeth, Lord Hillsborough and their friends set out on horseback across the hills for Castle Kerry.

The newspaper men who had come from London and Liverpool began looking around for places to sleep. Some of them bedded down with the crowds on the bluffs. A few persuaded the workmen in the telegraph shack to double up and make room for them there. Jack Mullaly walked as far as Knightstown, where he found a bed for himself in the tavern.

The next day two launches from the *Leopard* and one from the *Susquehanna* were brought under the stern of the *Niagara*. A mile and three-quarters of

From the bluff the islanders cheered the cable fleet.

cable were coiled from deck to deck. Then the *Willing Mind* came up behind and took on another mile.

After the loading had been completed the *Advice* maneuvered around and threw a towline to the first launch. The procession started off toward the shore.

Lord Hillsborough and his guests had galloped in from the castle and stationed themselves high up on the bluff near the telegraph shack. Right down to the water's edge, the whole harborside was teeming with people.

The little boats came in slowly and carefully, creeping along through the surf. At the end of four hours, they reached the shallow water of the beach.

Captain Pennock, one of the administrative officers on the *Niagara,* stood up in the first launch and seized the end of the cable. He raised it high above his head.

This was the signal for all the sailors in the other boats to stand up and hoist the cable to their shoulders. Captain Pennock jumped into the surf, waist-deep; the sailors followed after him. They began wading toward the shore.

Hundreds of cheering onlookers broke ranks and dashed into the water. Lord Morpeth was with them. He splashed right in and took hold of the cable just behind Captain Pennock. Everybody was anxious to help pull the magic cable.

For almost two hours they struggled toward the shore.

At last they stepped on dry land. Dripping and shaking themselves like shaggy dogs, they crossed the beach and climbed the bluff. In front of the telegraph shack, a stake had been driven into the ground.

Captain Pennock fastened the end of the line to the stake. Then he turned to Lord Morpeth who, soaked to the skin, was still close behind him. The two men grasped hands. The European end of the cable was safe.

Mr. Field, who hadn't gone into the water, stepped up quickly.

"Allow me to present Captain Pennock, Lord Morpeth," he said.

Lord Morpeth laughed. "I'm happy to meet you, Captain," he said, and they shook hands again.

"This, my lord," said Captain Pennock, not at all flustered, "is the betrothal of England and America. I hope in twenty days the marriage will be announced."

The introduction was followed by a long prayer, led by the rector of the parish. Then Lord Morpeth made a short speech, and after him Mr. Brooking, chairman of the executive committee of the Atlantic Telegraph Company, spoke for almost an hour. Finally it was Mr. Field's turn.

After thanking all the men for their help, Mr. Field invited the entire population of Valencia to visit him in America. He promised he would give them "a real American welcome."

They all cheered and promised to come.

By this time it was evening. The great day was over. The Lord Lieutenant went back to Dublin. Lord Hillsborough and his friends went back to Cork. The people of Valencia, tired and happy, went back to their homes. They all were full of plans to emigrate to America.

Mr. Field and his associates went with Captain Pennock and the men out to the ships.

The next morning, bright and early, the cable fleet got under way.

13

The Six Days

The *Niagara* barely got outside of the harbor before there was trouble with the cable. She had to go back and make a new start. Another whole day was lost before the cable-laying could proceed.

This time all went well and the *Niagara* sailed slowly westward.

A great deal had been learned about laying submarine telegraph lines since the *James Adger* took off on her first ill-fated voyage. The cable was coiled under water in a series of vats placed side by side amidships.

The line passed from the vats along the deck, then slid over a series of drums on the paying-out machine at the stern and fell by its own weight to the ocean bottom as the ship moved forward.

Close beside the machine were the brakes and a bell connected with the engine room. Men were stationed close together along the deck to keep watch on the cable. If they spotted the slightest imperfection in the line they yelled. Then the bell rang, the brakes clamped down, the ship's engine reversed, and the *Niagara* came to a dead stop. The *Niagara* was much more maneuverable than the *Adger* had been. She could back up or stop quite quickly.

After leaving Valencia Bay the *Niagara* moved steadily on, dropping cable at the rate of about two miles an hour.

At the end of five hours there was a real test of the cable's strength. The splice where the deep-sea cable had been joined to the shore end came up out of the vat and slithered across the deck.

The shore end of the cable had been heavily reinforced, for it would lie in shallow water where there were currents and waves. It was much thicker and stiffer than the deep-sea part, and much more difficult to pay out.

Would the splice hold under the strain?

Just as it reached the first drum it began to fray. A yell went up. The bell began to ring.

But before the *Niagara* could be brought to a stop, the half-broken cable had passed through the paying-out machine. It dangled by a thread between the wheels and the water.

Quick as a flash, a man went over the side on a rope. Hanging there, swinging back and forth, he was able to attach a hawser to the cable. Man, hawser and cable were hauled back on deck.

The telegraph line was still intact. The day was saved.

A new splice was made. The shore end, securely fastened to the lighter, deep-sea cable, was once more payed out. This time it dropped safely to the bottom of the sea.

"The splice . . . is lying on its ocean bed," wrote Jack Mullaly. "We are glad to get rid of it." The splice had been "a tough customer."

The telegraphers on the *Niagara* had been testing the current by exchanging messages with Valencia Bay. They reported that after the splice was made, communication was still intact.

Jack Mullaly sent a long telegram to James Gordon

From the vats the cable passed

Bennett, the owner of the New York *Herald*. Mullaly reported: "The cable is being payed out over the stern . . . and the ship is going at the rate of two miles an hour. We have just payed out the twelfth mile. . . . We can see the lights of the other steamers as they hover around us. . . ."

He signed the cable "J.M." and date-lined it "United States Frigate *Niagara* At Sea, August 8th, 1:00 P.M."

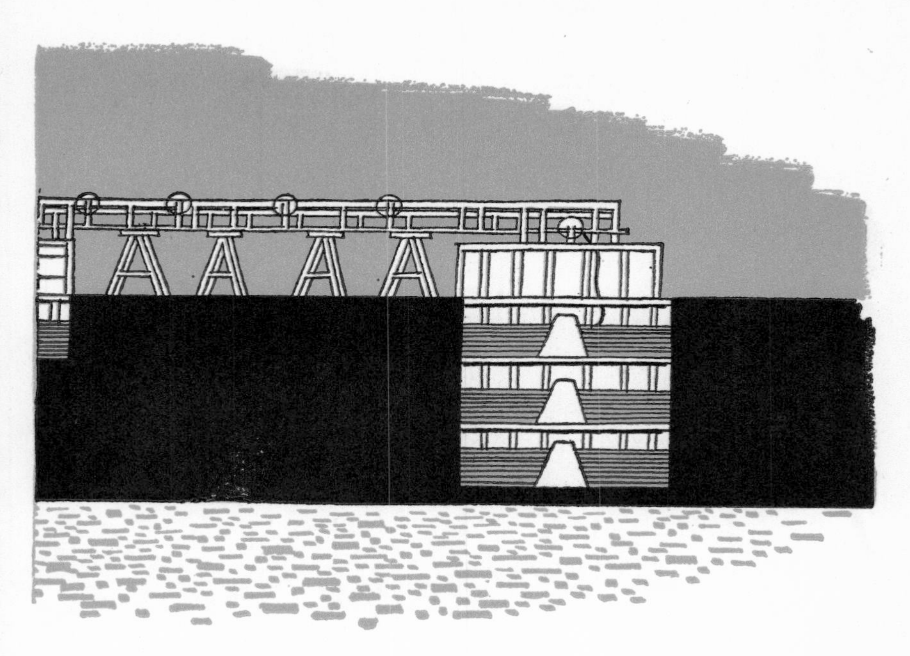

along the deck to the stern.

The message went by wire to London and by boat to New York. It was picked up by newspapers all over the world. It was probably the first ship-to-shore telegram ever published.

Day and night the people on the *Niagara* heard the rattle and the clatter of the paying-out machine. It was a deafening noise, but they didn't complain. They listened for it anxiously.

They sat up in their bunks and hammocks at night

to listen for it. Its constant racket was music to their ears.

If the "old coffee mill" stopped, even for an instant, all hands from cabin, wardroom and forecastle alike rushed on deck.

"It was more pleasing than the best opera ever produced by Italian, German, or any other composer," Mullaly wrote.

The telegraph shack had daily messages from Valencia Bay. The operators received news of the progress of the Sepoy Rebellion in far-off India. They transmitted the reports by signal to the British ships that circled round and round. For the first time in history, men at sea were kept in touch with the happenings on shore.

On the fifth day out, the bottom of the sea took a big dip. The fleet began to lay cable at 2,150 fathoms —the deepest water of that part of the Atlantic. Only two days more and they would reach the shallower "Telegraph Plateau."

Everybody in the cable fleet began to feel happy and relaxed. The passengers made bets at the mess table as to how long it would take to finish the job. The sailors made plans about their leave and started mending their shore togs.

One morning, while Mr. Field and Professor Morse

were taking a constitutional around the deck, with Jack Mullaly trotting behind, pad and pencil in hand, one of the telegraph operators came running toward them.

The "lightning" had failed. No more messages were coming in. There was no break in the cable, no kink, no coil, no fault. The line had just gone dead.

The *Niagara* stopped. The sailors and the workmen stood around, stunned.

"They talked of the cable as they would of a pet child," wrote Mullaly.

The engineers got together in the telegraph room. They were just as puzzled as the rest of the men, but they felt they had to do something.

"Maybe we ought to cut the cable," one of the men suggested to Captain Hudson.

The Captain turned to Mr. Morse. "What do you think, Professor?" he asked.

Professor Morse passed the question on. "Mr. Bright," he said, "as engineer-in-chief of this whole project, it's up to you to decide."

Charles Bright rubbed his chin. "We've already laid more than 300 miles of cable," he said. "If we cut it now, we'll lose all that. And what's more, if we go back it'll be too late to make a second try this year. I just don't know what to say. It's a dreadful responsibility."

Professor Morse put his hand on the young man's shoulder.

"Whatever you decide, Mr. Bright," he said, "we will stand by you."

Mr. Bright thought a moment.

"Then I say," he answered at last, "we must cut the cable." There was a moment of silence.

Suddenly, the telegraph instrument on the table began clicking. The messages were coming through again.

For those two hours and a half the line had been dead. No one has ever known why.

The word ran like wildfire through the ship. The crew cheered and the *Niagara* resumed speed.

But luck had run out. Early the next morning a high wind came up. The *Niagara,* heaving and tossing, battled with the heavy seas. The cable snapped in two. Nearly 350 miles of wire lay lost at the bottom of the Atlantic.

Sadly the telegraph fleet turned around and headed for England. The expedition of 1857, so gaily launched, had ended in disaster.

14

High Winds and Heavy Seas

The moment the *Niagara* made port, Mr. Field and his associates rushed up to London to make a report to the board of directors.

The directors were anything but happy about the outcome of the expedition. It certainly was not a good time to have lost almost 350 miles of costly cable at the bottom of the ocean.

Business was in a bad way. In America there had been a stock market crash. Stocks and bonds had gone down. Banks had failed. In England, too, money was tight.

Some of the old fogies blamed the new business panic on progress. "It's all these newfangled ideas," they said. "Poor people aren't saving their money any more. These so-called improvements have to be stopped! The old ways were better! We have to go back to them!"

As for a transatlantic submarine telegraph—that was against nature.

"A cable at the bottom of the sea," sneered the critics. "Poppycock. How do we know the sea *has* a bottom? Nobody's ever been down there, have they? It's just a new Yankee way to waste money."

Money! That was the trouble, for some of the money behind the venture had come from the taxpayers. And the British Admiralty and the American Congress were worried about the taxpayers' money. The two governments were ready to put a stop to the whole undertaking.

Even the directors of The Atlantic Cable Company were ready to call it quits. What was the use of throwing good money after bad!

"But we can't stop now," Mr. Field argued, when he was called on the carpet. "We've learned a lot from making this try. And we won't make the same mistakes again."

Mr. Everett, who had been chief ship's engineer on the *Niagara,* explained some of the improvements planned. The paying-out machine, for instance, was too heavy, and it couldn't change speed fast enough. He had already designed a new one. He had also figured out a way to keep the brakes from grabbing when it was necessary to slow down the paying-out of the cable.

Mr. Bright described a new kind of casing for the cable and a new way to coil it to get rid of kinks.

Professor Morse had ideas for simplifying his printing telegraph, so it would use less electricity.

"These things have to be done right away," said Mr. Field. "We have to use the winter months to refit the ships. We want to start out early in the spring this time. Then if we get into any trouble we'll still have the whole summer before us. We can count on good weather straight through to the end of August. We can keep on trying and trying until we get the cable laid."

"Mr. Field is right," said John Brett. "Look what happened to us when we laid the Channel cable. The line failed the first time, but we got it laid the next year. Laying a cable isn't a thing that can be done overnight. We all knew before we started that we were going into a gamble."

The directors gave in. They decided to dig down into their own pockets to make up the money that had already been lost. And they raised enough extra to guarantee another expedition.

When the British Admiralty and the American Congress learned that the directors were going to put up their own cash to cover the deficit, they agreed to provide the ships for the 1858 try.

Work on the improvements started at once. By the first week in May the new equipment was ready. The *Niagara* and the *Agamemnon* put in at Plymouth, England, and were refitted. Each took on half of the cable. Then they set out for Spain to make some tests in the waters of the Bay of Biscay and get all the gear in working order.

The first week in June they came back to Plymouth well satisfied. The tests had gone off in fine style. The second expedition was ready to get under way.

There had been a major change in the plans. The *Agamemnon* and the *Niagara,* each carrying half the cable, were to meet in mid-Atlantic. At the designated rendezvous, they would make a splice and start out in opposite directions.

The *Agamemnon* would head for Valencia Bay on the European side; and the *Niagara,* would make for Trinity Bay, Newfoundland, on the American side.

By this method, the troublesome shore ends of the cable would be laid last. If anything went wrong before either ship had laid 200 miles of line they would come back to the rendezvous, make a new splice and start out again. Each ship carried enough cable to make three tries.

The two ships would be in constant telegraph contact with each other. But no one on either shore would know what progress was being made until the whole job was done.

John Mullaly was again "official historian" for the *Niagara,* and a special correspondent from the London *Times* was on the *Agamemnon.* But there wouldn't be any fancy news flashes at sea this time. The two news hawks would have to wait to file their reports until they reached dry land.

Mullaly found plenty of old-timers when he joined the fleet. Captain Hudson was in command of the *Niagara.* Mr. De Sauty was once again in charge of the electrical force aboard the same ship, while Dr. Thomson had the same job on the *Agamemnon*. Mr. Canning, Mr. Everett, Mr. Bright and Professor Morse were also members of the expedition.

Of course Mr. Field was going along, too.

On June 10th, 1858, everything was ready. It was a perfect day for sailing. This time there were no picnics and no speeches. A short item buried in the pages of the London *Times* announced that the cable fleet had slipped quietly out of Plymouth harbor.

The third day out, the wind "freshened considerably towards evening and at night blew a perfect gale," according to Mullaly.

"Blowing heavy in squalls" . . . "a fresh gale" . . . "heavy sea with squalls" were the entries in the ships' logs. And Captain Dayman stated that it was the worst weather he had ever seen in the North Atlantic.

Driven off their course, the ships became separated. The *Agamemnon* and her consort both took a terrible beating. The *Niagara* was nearly run down by a merchant ship.

On June 23rd, thirteen days after leaving Plymouth, the *Niagara* arrived at the point designated for the rendezvous. She lay there pitching and tossing in the trough of the waves for three whole days.

But by the evening of the twenty-fifth the whole fleet had arrived and all of the ships were within hailing distance. The weather was perfect. The sky cleared and the stars came out. The officers visited back and forth in their dinghies. They decided to make the splice the next day.

The following morning there was no wind and the water was calm. The end of the cable stored in the *Niagara* was carried to the *Agamemnon*. After the splice had been made, the cable was dropped to the bottom of the ocean.

This done, the electric current was tested. It worked perfectly.

The *Agamemnon* turned toward the east, the *Niagara* toward the west. They began steaming away from the rendezvous, paying out the cable slowly and carefully.

Before they were even out of hailing distance, the line on the *Agamemnon* broke. The ships came together again, and a new splice was joined. Once again they headed away from each other.

The distance widened between the two ships. As

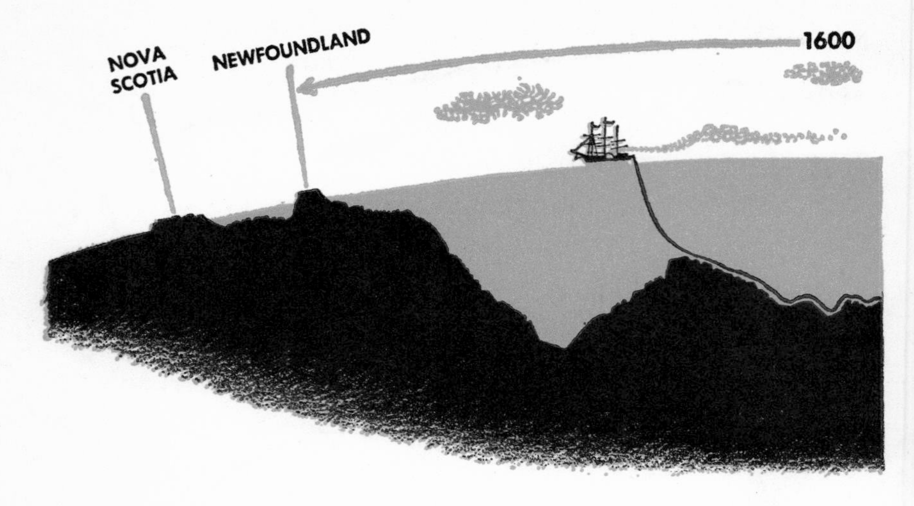

By its own weight it fell over

the dusk gathered, ten miles had been payed out between them. Two hours later, when the sun began to sink behind the horizon, they lost sight of each other.

As they drew farther and farther apart, the two ships sent constant messages to each other. Everything was "all right" at eight o'clock. Everything was "all right" at ten. By midnight thirty-one miles of cable had been laid, and everything was still "all right."

Then at ten minutes of one the *Agamemnon*'s end of the cable went dead. There was no way of knowing what had happened. For a while the telegraphers kept

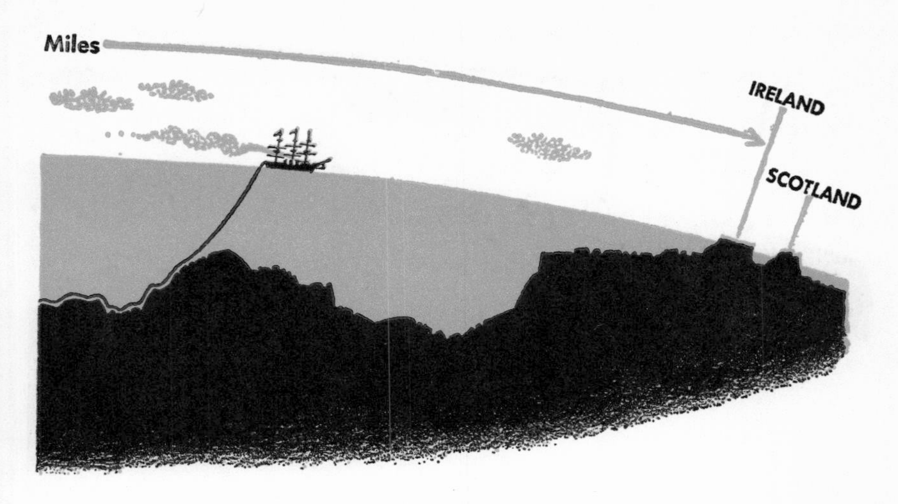

the drums to the ocean bottom.

on attempting to send messages to the *Niagara*. But the current remained dead, so the ship finally put about and made for the rendezvous point again.

Meanwhile, the *Niagara* was in a state of confusion. No more signals were coming through at that end of the cable either, for the cable had snapped somewhere on the ocean floor.

The big ship slowed down and stopped. All hands rushed on deck. The sailors gathered in little knots, talking it over. They had their own ideas about the operation.

"Our cable was running out all right," said one old fellow. "Why do we bother about the electricity? Just let's lay the wires and forget the other things."

The engineers and the scientists gathered in the telegraph room. They hoped that if they waited for a while "the lightning would start flowing again"—as had happened the year before.

Jack Mullaly, half-dressed, rolled out of his hammock and joined the anxious little group in the telegraph room.

One hour passed. Two hours.

"Three hours have passed," wrote Jack, "but the little magnetic needle in the electrician's office refuses to move."

There was no use waiting any longer. The *Niagara* put about and, according to plan, headed for the rendezvous, preparing to rewind the cable as she went.

But the cable wouldn't rewind. It broke.

The two ships together had lost thirty-two miles of cable. But there was still enough left in their holds to bridge the ocean.

Again, the telegraph squadron stood off in mid-Atlantic. For the third time a splice was made, and for the third time the ships parted company and headed in opposite directions.

On both ships everyone was tense and anxious. Aboard the *Niagara* "silence was commanded and no conversation allowed. Nothing was heard but the rattling of the machine as the cable was running out."

The scene on board the *Agamemnon* was much the same. "The whole of Monday night, neither Mr. Bright nor Mr. Canning quitted the machines for an instant. Toward the middle of the night, the speed at which the cable payed out slackened."

The engineers figured that the cable was creeping up the steep side of a submarine mountain. After an anxious hour, the cable began running out faster and faster. The mountain's peak had been reached and crossed. Now the line was running down hill.

Monday passed, then Tuesday. Two hundred miles of line lay safely on the bottom. Signals between the two ships flashed continuously back and forth.

On Wednesday, at a few minutes before one in the morning, the watchers on the deck of the *Agamemnon* saw the cable fly into the air twenty feet from the stern and snap in two. The loose end sank quickly below the surface. A howl of rage went up.

That was the end for the *Agamemnon*. She wasn't carrying enough cable to make another try. According to agreement, she headed for home.

On board the *Niagara* there was no way of knowing what had happened. The electric indicator in the telegraph room was motionless. Why had the line gone dead again?

For two anxious hours the *Niagara* waited. Then, according the plan, she put about. She started slowly east, rewinding the cable as she crept along. But her end of the cable broke, too.

Mr. De Sauty ordered a buoy launched to mark the spot. Then the *Niagara* gave up and made all speed for England.

The *Agamemnon* ran into heavy weather. For two weeks she tossed about in roaring gales. She ran out of coal. She lost her mainmast. It was mighty lucky that she wasn't trying to lay any cable in such a storm.

When at last the *Agamemnon* limped into port with only one sail, the news of the cable failure was there before her. The *Niagara*'s course had taken her around the tail end of the blow. She had been the first ship of the fleet to put in.

Once more Mr. Field, Mr. Bright, Professor Morse and Dr. Thomson hurried up to London. They got there just as The Atlantic Telegraph Company directors were meeting to dissolve the company.

While Mr. Field begged and pleaded, the chairman

resigned. The vice-chairman followed suit. It looked as though the Atlantic cable project, like the cable itself, had sunk to oblivion. However, Mr. Field had become a real fanatic. He tried everything. He reminded the directors that the fleet was still lying off Queenstown. He pointed out that extra cable—enough to replace the 300 miles that had been lost—was still available. He argued that it was only the middle of July, that there was still time to take advantage of the weather as had been planned.

Once more Mr. Field won.

The directors voted to make just one more try to lay the Atlantic submarine cable.

15

"If at First . . ."

The London papers had a field day when the news got out that the telegraph fleet was going to sea again.

They said the directors were fools and dupes—or else a bunch of rich men who wanted to get rid of their money by sinking it at the bottom of the sea. They openly referred to Mr. Field as a "Yankee gambler."

"It sounds as though we're sneaking away to commit an act of piracy," commented Jack Mullaly, "instead of sailing on a great international venture for the benefit of mankind."

He was still loyal and so were most of the men of the fleet.

The *Agamemnon* got a new mainmast, and her hull was patched up.

The extra miles of cable were brought over to Queenstown from England, and coiled on board the vessels. Then the ships coaled up.

It took just five days to finish their preparations.

There wasn't a moment to be lost. It was already the middle of July.

The fleet got under way on July 17th.

The *Niagara* arrived at the rendezvous on the evening of the 23rd. The weather was fine and clear.

Two of the other ships, the *Valorous* and the *Gorgon* had arrived by the 27th.

Then the sky became overcast and fog came down.

The next morning there lay the *Agamemnon* within hailing distance. It was a wonder that there hadn't been a collision in the thick weather.

Officers and men climbed into little boats and, rowing back and forth in a calm sea, made fast the two big ships with a hawser.

Then they carried the end of the *Niagara*'s cable to the *Agamemnon* and made a splice. The two halves of the telegraph cable were now joined in one continuous line—2,000 miles long.

A length of cable dangling loosely between the *Niagara* and *Agamemnon* was lowered carefully into the sea.

Two hundred ten fathoms were payed out while the fleet stood by. Then the signal *GO* was hoisted.

This was the last chance. The hawser connecting the two ships was cast loose, and for the fourth time the *Niagara* and the *Agamemnon* began moving slowly in opposite directions. They steamed farther and farther apart until they could no longer see each other.

Electrical signals were flashed back and forth. Deep down in the ocean bed, the cable that linked the two ships still held.

The night passed, and another day began. Mile after mile was laid, and the tiny thread of cable grew longer and longer.

Once, during the day, the current failed; but it mysteriously came back again.

Another night passed, and another day. Perhaps this time they were really going to make it.

A "small blow" hit the *Agamemnon,* but almost as quickly it died down.

The whale dived, carrying the cable with him.

A sailing ship crossed the *Niagara*'s course. By all the rules of the sea, she had the right of way over the steamer. She came bearing down under full sail.

The *Niagara* signaled desperately: "Laying cable. Can't veer."

When she was almost on them, the three-master got the signal, tacked, dipped and put about. It was a narrow squeak.

One day the lookout on the *Agamemnon* sighted a school of whales. At his cry, all hands rushed on deck, laughing and pointing and enjoying the antics of the big creatures as they sported and spouted.

Then one large whale left the flock and started straight for the *Agamemnon*. Cries and groans arose from the spectators as the monster came nearer and nearer. He swam right under the paying-out machinery. In a moment he was tangled in the cable. Then he dived, carrying it with him.

Nobody knew what to do. Bells rang. A dozen different orders flew back and forth.

Up to the surface came the whale. His tail was on one side of the line, his head on the other. He rolled and spouted and seemed all the time to be getting into a worse tangle.

The engineers got ready to put out boats. Even if the lifeboats capsized the cable had to be saved.

Then suddenly the huge creature shook himself free. Turning a somersault, he made off as fast as he could.

Anxiously, the engineers lowered men to examine the cable. It hadn't been hurt a bit. All the time the whale was dragging it about, the line hadn't gone dead.

The sea was getting shallower and shallower. On the opposite sides of the ocean, the ships were getting nearer land.

Then the *Niagara* sighted icebergs. There was nothing to do but go around them.

Hour after hour she steamed south, trying to escape the icebergs. Still the mountains of ice blocked her way.

The cable was running low. This big detour was using it up fast. The *Niagara* might not have enough line left to reach shore.

High above Trinity Bay, in a bunkhouse perched on a steep bluff overlooking the water, five men were sleeping soundly. The operators on the Newfoundland end of the New York and Newfoundland Telegraph Company had been keeping watch. They had been notified early in July that the cable fleet expected to leave Queenstown any day, and they had been alerted to watch for its arrival in America.

The little British ship *Porcupine* had been anchored just outside the bay under the command of Captain Otter, an old-timer. He was to pilot the *Niagara* through the rocky entrance of the harbor to a safe berth inside.

A month had passed, and still there was no sign of a ship. Then one night the men on watch all went to bed. Everybody had agreed that this expedition was going to be another fiasco. For the first time in weeks there was no lookout. The night was dark, and the surrounding forest quiet. The men slept soundly.

Suddenly there came a powerful pounding on the door.

One of the men jumped out of his bunk, grabbed a candle and ran for the door. Throwing it open, he stood there waving the unlighted candle.

"Where's the fire?" he asked grumpily.

There were three men outside—two sailors and a civilian, a middle-aged gentleman with a fine set of whiskers.

The gentleman's coat-tails were in shreds and he had lost his hat. The sailor's pants were torn. They hadn't been able to find the path in the dark, so they had scrambled up the side of the bluff through stones and brambles.

The man in the doorway rubbed his eyes at the sight.

"What do you want?" he asked again.

"I want you to get up," shouted the gentleman. "I'm

"Help us bring the telegraph cable ashore!"

Cyrus Field, and I want you to get up and help us bring the telegraph cable ashore."

"Bring the cable *ashore?"* the man repeated, rubbing his eyes again.

Then he came full awake.

"Hey, everybody! Get up!" he shouted. "The cable's here. We have to go down and take it ashore."

The others began clambering out of beds. They couldn't believe the news. They grabbed lanterns and, half-dressed, started running down the little path that led to the beach.

"The cable's here!" they yelled as they ran. "Hurrah! Hurrah!"

"Wait!" Mr. Field had to shout to make himself heard. Wait! One of you stay here with me. I want to send a telegram to New York."

"It's 2:00 A.M.," said one of the men. "The office in New York doesn't open till eight o'clock. Come on down to the beach."

And he started running again.

"Stop!" called Mr. Field in a voice of authority. "I'll write it out, and then I'll thank you to stay here and have the message sent at the earliest possible moment."

The two of them went back to the shack and Mr. Field dictated his message.

"Date it—Trinity Bay, Newfoundland, August 5th, 1858," he commanded. "It's to the Associated Press, New York: The Atlantic telegraph fleet sailed from Queenstown, Ireland, Saturday, July 17th, met in mid-ocean Wednesday, the 28th, made the splice at 1:00 P.M. Thursday the 29th. The *Agamemnon* and *Valorous* (her consort) bound to Valencia, Ireland; the *Niagara* and *Gorgon* (her consort) for this place, where they arrived yesterday. This morning the end of the cable will be landed. It is 1,696 nautical, or 1,950 statute miles from the telegraph house at the head of Valencia Harbor to the telegraph house at . . . Trinity Bay. For more than two-thirds of this distance, the water is over two miles in depth.

"The electrical signals sent and received through the whole cable are perfect."

Then came two paragraphs praising the officers and the engineers of the ships and describing the working of the paying-out machine.

"All have exerted themselves to the utmost to make the expedition successful and by the blessing of Divine Providence it has succeeded.

"Sign it Cyrus W. Field," he instructed.

Then, leaving the telegram with the excited operator, Mr. Field went quickly down the path to the shore. He wanted to be there when the Atlantic submarine cable was finally landed in America.

16

'Tis Done—
or Isn't It?

'Tis done! the angry sea consents,
The nations stand no more apart,
With clasped hands the continents
Feel throbbings of each other's heart.

Speed, speed the cable; let it run
A loving girdle round the earth,
Till all the nations 'neath the sun
Shall be as brothers of one hearth;

As brothers pledging, hand in hand,
One freedom for the world abroad,

One commerce over every land,
One language and one God.

The word of the cable's arrival spread as though by magic. People for miles around jumped out of bed and started celebrating as soon as they heard the news.

The hills came alive with bonfires. Men, women and children ran down to the shore, shouting and waving lighted lanterns. Little boats loaded with cheering natives, and with lights dangling from their masts, sprang up from nowhere and filled the bay. The landscape looked as though it were dotted with noisy fireflies.

All through the night the men on the *Niagara* were getting ready to land the cable.

Six small boats were lowered and connected by a hawser. Then the line was carefully let down over the side of the ship and coiled in the last of the six small boats. Each dory was manned by a crew of the best oarsmen from the *Niagara*.

The Captain was in the bow of the first boat. Fifteen of his officers were deployed behind.

As the rim of the sun showed over the sea the Captain gave the word. The crews bent to their oars, and the little procession shot forward. Cheers went up from the fishing smacks all around, and were echoed by the throngs lining the harbor.

Another hour passed before the cable boats were beached. Officers and men jumped to shore.

Mr. North, first lieutenant of the *Niagara,* was in the last boat with the cable. He picked up the end and started carrying it toward the Captain. But before Lieutenant North could hand over the cable, Mr. De Sauty grabbed it away from him and put the end in his mouth.

"It's alive!" he shouted. "I tasted the shock! The current's still coming!" And he handed the line to the Captain.

Taking a good grip on the end, the Captain crossed the beach and started up the hill. Behind him came officers and men in a single file, carrying the cable. As they pulled and strained, length after length uncoiled.

Straight up the bluff they went. Their trousers were torn by brambles, their jackets ripped by bushes. They were covered with tar from head to foot. But they didn't stop.

They reached the telegraph shack and attached the cable to the telegraph instrument. Almost immediately there came a clicking. A message was coming in, from across the ocean.

Six small boats were lowered and connected by a hawser.

"*Agamemnon* to *Niagara.* Knightstown, Ireland We have landed the cable."

Mr. De Sauty stepped up and put his hand on the telegraph key.

"Trinity Bay, Newfoundland. *Niagara* to *Agamemnon.* Congratulations on your good work. The Atlantic submarine cable is completed."

It was like a miracle. Men on two continents, eighteen hundred miles apart, had exchanged signals!

The sailors danced and slapped one another on the back. During the trip they had made a flag and sewed on it the word *Niagara.* Now they cut down a tree,

The crews bent to their oars and the procession shot forward.

lopped off the branches and raised it as a flagstaff.

John McMath, a sailor who had been on all the expeditions, shinnied up the pole and nailed the flag to the top.

"That'll tell 'em!" shouted John, waving his hat. "That'll tell 'em that it was the *Niagara*'s boys as laid the cable!" He slid down onto the shoulders of his shipmates.

News of the landing was flashed by telegraph everywhere. Salutes were fired in far-off St. Louis, in Boston, in Andover, in Philadelphia and Baltimore.

On the other side of the ocean, all business was

stopped on the London Stock Exchange. There were five minutes of silence for a prayer.

The next day the *Niagara,* accompanied by the English ships of the cable fleet, set out for New York. New Yorkers had been on holiday ever since Mr. Field's telegram had come to the Associated Press. People stopped work and danced in the streets. Volunteer fire departments held torchlight processions.

When the *Niagara* got to Sandy Hook, she was met by a fleet of tugboats. All the way up the bay, she was saluted by cannon fire. Whistles blew and crowds gathered on the wharves to welcome her.

The crew disembarked and marched up Broadway from the Battery to City Hall. Thousands of cheering citizens lined the streets.

A tremendous testimonial dinner was given for the telegraph directors and the officers of the fleet. Hundreds of the most distinguished people in the city came. There were dozens of long speeches and telegraphed messages of congratulation.

But though everybody was celebrating, the cable had not yet been thrown open to public use.

"Until the telegraph instruments are perfectly adjusted no communications can pass between the two continents," Mr. Field stated to the newspapers. "The electric currents are in good working order but Dr. Whitehouse, Professor Thomson and others are testing different methods of telegraphing before they decide on the most rapid mode for future use. Once the line has been thrown open for business, it wouldn't be possible to cut it off for experimenting, even for a short time."

People got more and more impatient. Ten days passed, and whispers began to circulate.

Then, on August 16th, it was suddenly announced that a message from Queen Victoria had been received. Its contents were published.

"To the President of the United States, Washington.

"The Queen desires to congratulate the President upon the successful completion of this great international work . . .

"The Queen is convinced that . . . the electric cable which now connects Great Britain with the United States will prove an additional link between the nations, whose friendship is founded upon their common interest and reciprocal esteem.

"The Queen has much pleasure in thus communicating with the President and renewing to him her wishes for the prosperity of the United States."

The President's answer was also widely reprinted.

"Washington City, August 16, 1858.

"To Her Majesty Victoria, the Queen of Great Britain:

"The President cordially reciprocates the congratulations of Her Majesty the Queen . . .

"It is a triumph . . . far more useful to mankind than was ever won . . . on the field of battle. May the Atlantic Telegraph . . . prove to be a bond of peace and friendship . . . and an instrument destined by Divine Providence to diffuse religion, civilization, liberty, and law throughout the world.

(*signed*) JAMES BUCHANAN."

The President and the Queen and the people of both countries were hoping, as men have always hoped, that better understanding would come about if people could communicate directly.

In New York City, the morning after the Queen's message was received, 100 guns were fired in Central Park at daybreak, and again at 12:00 noon. The buildings were decorated with flags; the bells of all the churches were rung, and people crowded in for special services.

That night the whole city was lit up.

In England the Queen announced that she had knighted Charles Bright and was giving decorations and titles to several of the officers and engineers who had taken part in the expedition. At the Crystal Palace there was another big mass meeting in honor of Mr. Field and the officers of the ships of the cable fleet.

But in Trinity Bay the operators weren't so happy. The electric current seemed to be fading.

As Henry Field later wrote, "That very day that a whole city rose up to do honor to the Atlantic Telegraph and its author, it gave its last throb and that first cable was thenceforth to sleep forever silent in its ocean grave."

The Atlantic submarine cable had mysteriously gone dead.

17

The British Nearly Go to War

The crowds which had gathered in the Crystal Palace to celebrate the cable's triumph were the first to hear of the cable's failure. They streamed out of the hall into the streets to spread the news. The reporters rushed to get the story on the front pages of the morning editions.

Instead of bringing peace, the submarine telegraph started a war of words.

"Was the Atlantic Cable a Humbug?" headlined a Boston newspaper.

"The Queen's message was a fraud," screamed the New York dailies. "It was written beforehand by the double-dealing English."

"A fishy transaction!" wrote an editor in Dublin. "Very like a whale!"

"It was a stock speculation!" read the London story. "A Yankee trick!"

"It was a hoax! A fake!" sneered the people on both sides of the Atlantic. "The cable was never laid."

During the experimental period, London Stock Exchange reports had been printed in New York within a few hours of closing. Stories of the Bombay mutiny and the peace treaty with China had been reported in America just three days after they were published in England. Sailings of ships from Queenstown and English weather information had been received immediately in America. And the account of a steamship collision off Cape Grace was a page one story in the London *Times*.

This information could have been sent only by cable.

But the public didn't care about the facts. The public was angry. People felt they had been duped.

Like the wire itself, lying at the bottom of the Atlantic, The Atlantic Telegraph Company was sunk. It looked as though no amount of grappling with the problem would ever bring it to the surface again.

But the excitement about the "Grand Hoax" soon died down. Americans had other things to talk about. The bitter feeling between the North and the South grew stronger every day. The settlers in the West were demanding territory status and statehood, but Congress kept on stalling. The Southerners voted for slavery in the West. The Northerners voted against it. They were determined to keep slavery from spreading.

The Westerners grew impatient. They began to talk about forming their own states, leaving the Union and setting up a nation of their own.

The Americans weren't interested in an international project like the cable. They turned their backs on Europe and busied themselves with what was going on at home.

As for Cyrus Field, there was nothing for him to do but sit still and hope. Every now and then he'd look at the globe in his library. He couldn't find anyone to listen to talk about the submarine telegraph.

After Civil War broke out between the North and South, America was not a bit concerned about links with other countries. Consequently the English turned their backs on the unreliable New World. They began laying cables on their own side of the Atlantic—under the Red Sea, the Mediterranean, the Aegean, the North Sea, and up the Scandinavian fjords.

Within three years thirty-four lines had "slipped to rest on the ocean bed." The British had plenty of things to talk about besides America.

But the Old World couldn't isolate America for long. In Europe, business had been booming. Suddenly it fell off. One of Great Britain's most important industries, the making and exporting of cotton cloth, was hit hard. Most of England's raw cotton had come from the Southern states—the states that had seceded from the Union to form the Confederacy.

The Union government threw an embargo around the Southern ports, and the Confederates couldn't get their cotton out to England.

British factories began to shut down. Thousands of families were thrown out of work. It looked as though England would have to help the Confederacy in order to keep British people from starving.

Confederate envoys shipped for London in British ships to negotiate a treaty. American naval vessels seized the English ships and kidnapped the Confederates. They were practically committing piracy—but there was a war on.

England demanded an explanation.

Feeling ran high on both sides of the ocean. Great Britain got ready to recognize the Confederate states and send money and ships.

Then President Lincoln issued the Emancipation Proclamation. Since Great Britain had just freed the slaves in her own colonies, she couldn't very well go into the war on the side of the Confederacy. She would be aiding a nation which was fighting to preserve slavery.

Queen Victoria and her advisers did an about-face. They decided to stay neutral. They accepted the apologies of the Federal government.

"All this might have been prevented by a single word of explanation," commented the London *Times*. "We nearly went to war with the United States because we had no telegraph across the Atlantic."

This was what Mr. Field had been waiting for. Once again people were thinking about a submarine cable.

18

Let the Electric Telegraph Be Laid

Hugest of all Great God's Works
That swim the ocean stream.

Daniel Gooch sat in his London office.

On his desk lay the reports of the Great Eastern Steamship Company. They told the story. The *Great Eastern,* the big ship, had been a big failure.

Every year since she had been launched the *Great Eastern* had cost the stockholders more than a hundred thousand dollars. Twice she had been advertised for sale. And twice nobody had bought her.

That very afternoon, by order of the Cunard Line, the chief mortgagee, she had been put up at auction in the cotton room of the Liverpool Exchange. Joseph Cunard himself had been the auctioneer. The price had been pegged at $500,000.

There had been no takers. The company still had the ship on its hands.

Another auction was planned to take place in three weeks' time. The *Great Eastern* would be sold to the highest bidder regardless of price.

She had certainly not been a lucky ship, Gooch thought to himself. He remembered how proud his hero Brunel had been of her.

Brunel was dead now. In a way, it might be said that the big ship had killed him. Shortly after she was launched, the forward funnel had blown out of the ship with a shattering explosion. The news killed Brunel, already suffering from a stroke. People said he died of a broken heart.

It was probably true, thought Gooch. Anyhow, Brunel would have broken his heart over the *Great Eastern* sooner or later. Her history was just a list of disasters—one after the other. She had run into storms, killed members of her crew, run down other ships and crashed into docks. Just the preceding summer, on a trip to New York, her bottom had been ripped on shoals off Montauk Point, Long Island. This little mishap had cost the shareholders thousands of pounds more in repairs.

Brunel had been spared all this. On the other hand if he'd been around perhaps he could have made his ship a success. He'd done it before with his other enterprises.

Gooch pushed the papers aside. No use going back over things—he had to hurry. He had an appointment at the club with Thomas Brassey, a fellow director in the company that owned the *Great Eastern*. Brassey was an Irishman, the son of a man who had made a fortune promoting railroads all over the world. The son had increased the fortune until he was the richest mogul in the British Isles. He was used to thinking in millions—millions of changeable French francs, millions of shaky American dollars and millions of stable English pounds.

Brassey was dining with Cyrus Field, the American promoter who had come to England to revive interest in the Atlantic submarine cable. Brassey was just the kind of fellow who would take up Cyrus Field. And

Field was another one like Brunel, thought Gooch. Once he got an idea he didn't give up.

The three men—Gooch, Brassey and Field—got along famously.

At first the talk was all about the war in America. The United States government was finally winning, said Field. The battles of Gettysburg and Vicksburg had turned the tide. Abraham Lincoln was sure to be reëlected. President Lincoln felt that the future of both America and England depended on their friendship.

Businessmen in the British Isles felt that way too, Field went on.

"What about the cable project?" asked Gooch.

He'd met great encouragement from all the people he'd talked to, Mr. Field answered. Of course, there was the little matter of money.

By this time the roast beef was on the table.

Thomas Brassey picked up his knife and fork and banged them on the table.

"Let the cable be laid between England and America," he boomed.

The other people in the room looked up. They wondered what the noise was about.

"Let us spin a cobweb between the two countries," said Brassey. "I'll head the list of cash subscribers."

Mr. Field laughed. "Well, I suppose that takes care of the money for the Atlantic Cable Company," he said. "And now there's only the matter of ships."

He began talking about Brunel. He told of meeting the little giant on the train so long ago. At that time the great engineer had said the *Great Eastern* was the only ship capable of laying the cable.

Daniel Gooch thought quickly.

"The Great Eastern Company is in trouble," he said. "Maybe we could persuade them to do something for us. What do you think, Brassey?"

Before dinner was over, the three men had hatched a plan to acquire the huge ship.

They expected to have to pay about $400,000; but when the auction was held, there was no competition. The *Great Eastern* was knocked down for about $125,000.

Gooch and Brassey and a couple of their friends were the new owners.

A howl went up from the old shareholders. They claimed that they were being swindled by the directors of their own management. This time they didn't even have the satisfaction of calling it a Yankee trick.

But nothing could be done to stop the transaction.

Only the Great Eastern *was capable of laying the cable.*

It was all legal. Big share owners and little share owners were all forced out. Gooch and his partners had taken title to the bankrupt ship.

Quickly, Gooch set up a new organization—a company to operate the *Great Eastern* as a cable layer. Brassey paid off the creditors a few cents on the dollar. Some of them didn't mind too much, for they were taken into the new company and given big blocks of stock.

Today a deal such as this would probably be investigated, but it was considered "pretty smart" in those days. The shareholders were the only ones who complained. The rest of the public was delighted.

Now the Atlantic submarine telegraph cable looked as if it were a sure thing.

19

To Spin a Thread of Thought

Early in 1865 the *Great Eastern* lay anchored at Sheerness, at the mouth of the Thames. The huge ship had been stripped of some of her elegant trappings, and her fourth funnel had been taken out to make room for cable-storage vats. There were three of these vats—one fore, one in the main hold and one aft. Together they weighed 2,000 tons and could take care of nearly 3,000 miles (7,000 tons) of cable.

Approximately eight thousand tons of coal were stored in the ship's hold, and one section of her deck was transformed into a corner of an English farmyard. Enough cows, calves, pigs and chickens were penned up there for the entire crew of 500 to enjoy fresh milk, eggs and meat during the trip.

The *Great Eastern* didn't look like a pleasure ship any more. In her stern the huge paying-out machine had been installed with all the latest improvements. Beside it was another contraption especially designed for rewinding the cable.

Halfway up the deck a grapple had been set up. It looked like an out-sized fishing line with powerful iron fingers instead of a hook. These fingers could be lowered into the water and could go groping about at the bottom of the sea for a lost cable.

The cable itself had been manufactured at Greenwich, England, in the works of the Telegraph and Maintenance Company which had absorbed the old firm of Glass, Elliot and Company. The Telegraph and Maintenance Company had full charge of the cable laying. Mr. Canning was in charge of the engineering department, and Mr. De Sauty was head of the electrical department.

Mr. Field, Professor Thomson and Mr. Varley, chief electrician for the Atlantic Telegraph Company, were going along on the *Great Eastern*. But their job was merely to observe and make suggestions if asked, and see that the conditions of the contract were complied with.

When the operation was complete, Mr. Canning and his co-workers would hand over the finished telegraph to Mr. Field and step out of the picture. Everybody agreed that this was a good arrangement. They all felt that there had been "too many cooks" on the former trips.

The inside of the new cable was made of copper so pure that a very light electrical charge could pass through it.

The casing was made of steel wire covered with gutta-percha instead of iron. The method of making steel wire in quantity had been perfected since the expedition of 1858. This made the new cable, though much thicker than the old, more flexible and easier to coil.

At Greenwich the finished cable was loaded length by length onto two barges and towed down to Sheerness to the *Great Eastern*.

"The big leviathan swallowed shipload after shipload as though she could never be satisfied," wrote an enthusiastic reporter for the Railway News.

There were plenty of reporters on hand at Sheer-

The cable was loaded onto the huge ship from barges.

ness, and all of them—English, French, Russian and German—had put in bids to sail.

But only one was invited.

The lucky man was William Howard Russell, the most famous war correspondent of the day. He was appointed official historian.

Russell, an Irishman who worked for the London *Times,* had reported the Crimean War and the Charge of the Light Brigade. His dispatches had inspired a nurse named Florence Nightingale to set up the first regular field hospital in the world. The English had dubbed him "Crimea" Russell.

At last everything was ready. The Telegraph and Maintenance Company gave a big farewell dinner for Mr. Field. They invited Daniel Gooch and all the officers, scientists and engineers who were going along on the expedition. Even Charles Francis Adams, the United States Ambassador to the Court of St. James's, was present.

It was a wonderful evening. The Americans toasted the English. The English toasted the Americans.

The next morning, with the cable safely stowed aboard, the *Great Eastern* made ready to haul up her seven-ton anchor. The anchor chain, every link of which weighed seventy pounds, was attached to a capstan in her stern.

A sailor with a fiddle climbed on top of the capstan. Two hundred sailors manned the spokes. The rest of the crew climbed up to the top of the two square-rigged mainmasts.

The fiddler began to play. The men on the cross-

To the fiddler's tune the sailors pushed the capstan round.

beams began to sing. The boatswain piped the signal. The sailors at the winch began pushing. Straining and panting and keeping time to the music, they turned the capstan round and round, winding up the anchor.

The anchor came up. The starting gun was fired.

The *Great Eastern* gave one great big shiver. Black smoke poured out of her three funnels, and her paddles began to revolve. Slowly the big ship moved out to sea.

20

The Battle of the Century

The *Great Eastern* did not attempt to navigate the passage into Valencia Bay. She lay in Bantry Bay while a small steamer, the *Caroline,* took the shore end of the cable toward Valencia. In shallow Foilhummerum Bay, the cable was passed over a bridge of twenty-five yawls. Then it was landed, hauled up the cliffs and made fast in a new, more modern telegraph station.

During the years that had passed since the *Niagara* had visited the island, the people of Valencia had gone back to their old humdrum way of living. Now they once again gathered on the bluffs and the beach to picnic and celebrate. The Knight of Kerry was present with the same swarms of notables and newspapermen and the same cheering crowds.

When the ceremonies were finally over, the *Caroline* put out to sea again with the cable end. A dispatch was forwarded to the *Great Eastern* to come round with all speed from Bantry Bay.

The next day the shore end of the cable was spliced to the cable stored aboard the *Great Eastern*. Her two consort ships, the *Terrible* and the *Sphinx,* ranged alongside. According to Russell they "sent their crews into the shrouds and up to the tops to give her a parting cheer, delivered their friendly broadsides with vigor, and received a similar greeting."

Slowly the *Great Eastern* moved ahead, paying out cable over the machine at her stern as she went. It was the twenty-third of July, 1865—a Sunday. The sound of church bells ringing in Valencia came floating out over the water. This was a good omen, declared the happy sailors.

The *Great Eastern* plowed comfortably along, powered sometimes by her great paddle wheels and sometimes by her twin-screw propeller. She was steady as a rock. The people on board said they "felt as safe as though they were on land."

However, up in the testing room forward, where Mr. Canning and his engineers were on duty, there was a feeling of tension. The leaders of the expedition had an extra reason for wanting to get the cable laid and working this time.

In the United States the Western Union Telegraph Company had come forward with a plan to connect America with Europe in a new way. They proposed to extend their transcontinental land line across Canada into Alaska, which still belonged to Russia. Then the line would cross over the Aleutians and under the narrow Bering Sea to Siberia, and so through Russia to the rest of Europe.

They had already started work on the Siberian end. They thought they could complete the entire line within two years. A race was on between the Western Union and the Atlantic Cable Company.

Mr. Canning and his assistants tested and retested the cable. They exchanged frequent signals with Valencia. They kept constant watch on the insulation- and resistance-testing machines and the galvanometer. The galvanometer was an invention of Professor Thomson. Its tiny ray of light, reflected from a mirror, indicated that the cable was live and the current flowing.

Twice the light glided out of bounds and vanished —a warning that current was escaping from the cable. A fault had occurred in the line. Each time the watchers quickly signaled the engine room, and the *Great Eastern* stopped short. On both occasions some of the cable had to be brought up from the ocean bottom before the fault was spotted.

The engineers were able to cut out the bad piece and make a new splice. Thereupon the *Great Eastern* moved forward again, laying line as before.

After the second scare Russell, the reporter, did a little snooping. He was looking for a story.

He ferreted out the fact that in each instance a short spike of copper had been found sticking into the gutta-percha covering.

Had the spike been put there on purpose? Could this be sabotage? He suggested that someone with a grudge might purposely have weakened the cable as it uncoiled.

Captain Anderson called a meeting of passengers and crew. He and Mr. Canning ordered the men to rip the pockets out of the coveralls which they wore when they went down into the vats. They set a twenty-four-hour watch to frisk the men for "foreign substances" when they came to work. The "guards" were also to inspect every inch of cable as it uncoiled and ran across the deck toward the paying-out machine.

Mr. Field, Mr. Gooch, Dr. Thomson and several trustworthy young gentlemen were appointed shift foremen.

For two days the entire ship was in a state of excitement. Every two hours another sleuth went down into the vats and came up two hours later, tired and covered with tar.

The expedition crossed the halfway mark. Eleven hundred and eighty-six miles of cable had been safely payed out since the *Great Eastern* left Valencia.

On the morning of the eleventh day, the galvanometer indicated another fault in the line. This time Mr. Field himself had been on duty. He and one of the other men had spied a fault in the cable as it was payed out, but they had been unable to give the alarm in time to check the cable before it slid into the sea.

Nobody could have tampered with the wire while Mr. Field was watching. The engineers began to suspect that the cable might contain the elements of its own destruction. What had looked like deliberate damage might well have been an accident due to some defect in the design of the cable's protective covering.

There was nothing to do but reverse the direction of the ship and pick up the cable from the ocean bottom until they came to the faulty piece. This time, though, the cable snapped in two while they were pulling it up. It had become frayed where it rubbed against the bow of the ship.

After a conference Mr. Canning decided to grapple for the lost cable. The grapple, a five-armed anchor with curved toothlike ends, was lowered over the side of the vessel. Length after length of the line flew over the drum until the men calculated that the iron fingers were close to 5,000 feet under the dark waters. It was a weird sight—the biggest ship in the world fishing at the bottom of the vast Atlantic Ocean for the end of a cable four inches thick.

"It was an elephant, feeling with its trunk to catch a cobweb," wrote Russell.

All night long the iron fingers of the grapple groped over the ocean bed, while the great ship tried to keep to the course. Hours passed.

Suddenly at 6:00 A.M. the next morning the iron fingers caught on something. Was it the cable?

Anxiously the men began hauling in the line. Their

instruments soon confirmed that they had indeed caught the cable.

The grappling line was nearly two-thirds of the way up when it broke. Hook, line and cable fell back into the ocean.

By this time a blanket of fog was enveloping the cable fleet. The *Great Eastern* veered around, blowing her fog horns to warn the *Terrible* of her change of position. The next day a buoy was thrown overboard to mark the place where the cable had sunk. But continuing fog and unfavorable winds prevented the *Great Eastern* from grappling for the cable again. She drifted helplessly while the *Terrible* stood by to mark the position of the buoy.

For two more days the *Great Eastern* drifted blindly waiting for the weather to clear. On the third day the sun shone briefly and the buoy was sighted. The big ship maneuvered until she was in position. Then another grappling line was lowered. This attempt was no more successful than the first. Again the line broke before the cable was raised to the top of the ocean.

Mr. Canning was everywhere—giving orders, encouraging the men, even taking a hand at the grapple.

On the third try the grappling line broke again. This time the engineers couldn't repair it. They had run out of wire and hemp.

Even Mr. Canning gave up.

The *Terrible* was short of coal. Even the enormous supply in the bunkers of the *Great Eastern* was low.

The *Terrible* made for Newfoundland under sail. The *Great Eastern* headed straight for England.

Back in Valencia, of course, no message had been received since the cable snapped. Nothing had been heard of the cable fleet for almost two weeks. Were the big ship and her consorts lost at sea?

The bell at Lloyd's was tolled, and the names of the *Great Eastern* and the *Terrible* were struck off the roster. Once more the public turned against the Atlantic cable.

Then the big ship made port.

The fickle public made a switch. The *Great Eastern* was suddenly the greatest ship afloat. Mr. Field was a hero; Daniel Gooch was a smart businessman. And the Telegraph and Maintenance Company was the darling of the press.

"We'll do it for sure next year. The gamble has now gone out of laying the cable," said Mr. Field to the reporters. And he managed to secure additional funds amounting to $40,000 to show that he meant what he said.

"There's no more risk to laying a cable than to throwing a bridge across the Upper Nile in Tanganyika, and that's been done," said Mr. Gooch. Then he produced $80,000 out of his own funds to back up his words.

Thomas Brassey put up a big sum, and several other businessmen signed sizable checks which they handed over to Gooch and Brassey.

"We'll guarantee to lay the cable next year," promised Richard Glass. And sure enough, in the spring of 1866, smoothly and uneventfully the *Great Eastern* strung 1,800 miles of new cable from Ireland to Newfoundland.

The big ship then turned around, went back six hundred miles, grappled thirty times, and picked up the 1865 cable.

It was still live!

Mr. Canning, Mr. Field and Daniel Gooch were standing on the deck of the *Great Eastern* when the cable was tested.

They looked at each other for a moment, then hurriedly turned away. None of the tough old fellows wanted the others to see the tears in his eyes.

When they landed the 1865 cable at Newfoundland, they found Professor Morse waiting for them. Without saying a word, the four men clasped hands.

They had won their great gamble. Two cable lines now stretched from Ireland to Newfoundland.

Europe and America were linked together by a living thread.

21

A Changed World

A new era in communications had begun.

As soon as the first Atlantic cable was finished, messages began flying between London and New York by way of Newfoundland and Ireland.

From England the Queen sent greetings to President Andrew Johnson, and the White House replied with congratulations to Buckingham Palace.

One of the first news stories cabled from the United States to Europe reported that the State of Tennessee had been readmitted to the Union.

Closing stock quotations were exchanged between the Brussels Grain Market, the Paris Bourse, the London Exchange and Wall Street. The public now had plenty of proof that the electromagnetic telegraph was indeed safely laid and in working order.

The Atlantic telegraph was in business. The two cables together carried close to 4,800 words per day. At $1.25 a word, this added up to a considerable sum. The Atlantic Cable Company was a success.

Within three years a new cable combine was formed under Julius Reuter, of the European news agency, Reuters. The new company chartered the *Great Eastern* to lay a cable from Brest, on the west coast of France, to the little French islands of St. Pierre and Miquelon off the coast of Newfoundland. From there it went straight into Boston.

Old Dan Gooch (now Sir Daniel) helped finance this new cable, and he went along to see it land.

The following year a cable was run from Lisbon, Portugal, to Pernambuco (Recife), Brazil. The distance was much greater than that covered by the first cable, and the ocean bed was much more uneven.

By the turn of the century there were as many as twenty-one transatlantic lines connection Europe and

America. One of these was German—from Bremen to New York. Two were French. The others, like the first cable, were jointly laid by the United States, Canada and Great Britain.

Before too long the most remote parts of the world were connected by cable—South Africa with London, Japan with the United States.

In 1928 a direct wire was laid under the Pacific Ocean from British Columbia in Canada to Australia. The distance between these points was almost twice as long as the distance between Ireland and Newfoundland.

Then came a new development. By the end of World War I, wireless telephony had been made practical. And before many years had passed, people could actually hear each other's voices across the Atlantic. They began to feel that sending dots and dashes over wires was slow and clumsy for transmitting messages.

Cable laying seemed to be going out of style.

Then came World War II. Transatlantic radio telephony might become unreliable. It might be intercepted or jammed. Even in peacetime it was often affected by the weather. But although both the Allies and the Axis tried to put them out of commission, the old telegraph cables at the bottom of the sea kept right on working.

Why not lay an Atlantic telephone cable?

There were new kinds of insulating plastics, much better than the original gutta-percha and tar. The method of spinning copper wire had been improved. The science of electronics had made great strides.

However, one problem still plagued the scientists —the same problem that had puzzled the original cable layers. An electric current faded after it traveled a certain distance.

The telephone experts had discovered a way to cope with this in long-distance telephony on land. They built relays, or boosters, at short distances along the circuit. These boosters worked perfectly for land circuits. However, the most important part of such a booster was the vacuum tube. And no vacuum tube was small enough or strong enough to be encased in a cable and dropped to the bottom of the sea.

Big companies with billions of dollars and millions of stockholders started working on the project. They engaged some of the greatest scientists and engineers and hired highly trained assistants, who went to work on the problem in completely equipped modern laboratories. Finally the researchers came up with a practical booster.

Once more Britain, Canada and the United States prepared to go ahead with a joint cable-laying project.

In the summer of 1955 the British post-office cable ship *Monarch* started shuttling back and forth between Oban, Scotland, and Clarenville, Newfoundland.

The cable layer was not a great, gaudy queen of the sea like the *Niagara* or the *Great Eastern*. But she was scientifically designed to do her job of laying cable and picking it up, when necessary, for repairs.

A good deal of the gamble has been taken out of cable laying, but it is a big adventure even today. Whales and other big fish still get tangled in the lines. Also, the lines get caught in fish nets and are hauled out and cut by fishermen, just as happened with Professor Morse's experiment. Sometimes the cable breaks without anybody knowing why. Added to everything else, and despite our advances in scientific knowledge, many secrets remain hidden at the bottom of the sea.

But the cable that slid over the *Monarch's* paying

out machinery was far different from the first iron-covered line, insulated only with gutta-percha, which first carried the lightning.

The modern cable comes in four sizes. For the shallow water it is thick and heavily armored, two and one-half inches in diameter, and weighs almost nine pounds a foot. The deep-water cable tapers down to an inch and a quarter and weighs only one pound per foot. Inside the cable is a line of purest copper wire, through which thirty-six voices can flow simultaneously. This is covered with three copper tapes insulated with a newly invented plastic, and then covered by six copper return tapes. This core is protected by copper tape, cotton tape, twenty-four cotton-covered armor wires, and three layers of jute.

And inside each cable at forty-mile intervals are fifty-one "carrier-repeaters," each carrying a three-stage electron-tube amplifier. Each carrier-repeater is made up of three sections, containing capacitors, resistors and electron tubes. The sections are joined together by short steel springs so that the repeaters can bend around the drums of the cable-laying machinery and straighten out again as the cable sinks.

Technicians believe that these carrier-repeaters can

continue to operate at the bottom of the sea for twenty years.

By the end of September 1958, two such telephone cables, one for transmission in each direction, lay safely on the ocean floor. Now government leaders, businessmen and just friends and families on both sides of the Atlantic could talk directly to each other by simply picking up a telephone. Their voices traveled 2,250 miles under the sea. Thirty-six separate conversations could be carried on at the same time.

Almost immediately plans were made for more cables. A second Atlantic telephone project got under way—this connects the American continent directly with the continent of Europe, by way of Penmarch in France. Telephone cable-laying operations were begun in all parts of the world. Soon people in all lands would be talking to each other around the globe.

By this time exactly one hundred years had passed since the *Niagara* placed the first unreliable cable on the telegraph plateau and Queen Victoria signaled a message of friendship to President Buchanan by electromagnetic telegraph.

Index

Index

Index

Index

Index

LANDMARK BOOKS

1 **The Voyages of Christopher Columbus** by Armstrong Sperry
2 **The Landing of the Pilgrims** by James Daugherty
3 **Pocahontas and Captain John Smith** by Marie Lawson
4 **Paul Revere and the Minute Men** by Dorothy Canfield Fisher
5 **Our Independence and the Constitution** by Dorothy Canfield Fisher
6 **The California Gold Rush** by May McNeer
7 **The Pony Express** by Samuel Hopkins Adams
8 **Lee and Grant at Appomattox** by MacKinlay Kantor
9 **The Building of the First Transcontinental Railroad** by Adele Nathan
10 **The Wright Brothers** by Quentin Reynolds
11 **Prehistoric America** by Anne Terry White
12 **The Vikings** by Elizabeth Janeway
13 **The Santa Fe Trail** by Samuel Hopkins Adams
14 **The Story of the U. S. Marines** by George Hunt
15 **The Lewis and Clark Expedition** by Richard L. Neuberger
16 **The Monitor and the Merrimac** by Fletcher Pratt
17 **The Explorations of Père Marquette** by Jim Kjelgaard
18 **The Panama Canal** by Bob Considine
19 **The Pirate Lafitte and the Battle of New Orleans** by Robert Tallant
20 **Custer's Last Stand** by Quentin Reynolds
21 **Daniel Boone** by John Mason Brown
22 **Clipper Ship Days** by John Jennings
23 **Gettysburg** by MacKinlay Kantor
24 **The Louisiana Purchase** by Robert Tallant
25 **Wild Bill Hickok Tames the West** by Stewart H. Holbrook
26 **Betsy Ross and the Flag** by Jane Mayer
27 **The Conquest of the North and South Poles** by Russell Owen
28 **Ben Franklin of Old Philadelphia** by Margaret Cousins
29 **Trappers and Traders of the Far West** by James Daugherty
30 **Mr. Bell Invents the Telephone** by Katherine B. Shippen
31 **The Barbary Pirates** by C. S. Forester
32 **Sam Houston, The Tallest Texan** by William Johnson
33 **The Winter at Valley Forge** by Van Wyck Mason
34 **The Erie Canal** by Samuel Hopkins Adams
35 **Thirty Seconds Over Tokyo** by Ted Lawson and Bob Considine
36 **Thomas Jefferson** by Vincent Sheean
37 **The Coming of the Mormons** by Jim Kjelgaard
38 **George Washington Carver** by Anne Terry White
39 **John Paul Jones** by Armstrong Sperry
40 **The First Overland Mail** by Robert Pinkerton
41 **Teddy Roosevelt and the Rough Riders** by Henry Castor
42 **To California by Covered Wagon** by George R. Stewart
43 **Peter Stuyvesant of Old New York** by Anna and Russel Crouse
44 **Lincoln and Douglas** by Regina Z. Kelly
45 **Robert Fulton and the Steamboat** by Ralph Nading Hill
46 **The F.B.I.** by Quentin Reynolds
47 **Dolly Madison** by Jane Mayer
48 **John James Audubon** by Margaret and John Kieran
49 **Hawaii** by Oscar Lewis
50 **War Chief of the Seminoles** by May McNeer
51 **Old Ironsides, The Fighting *Constitution*** by Harry Hansen
52 **The Mississippi Bubble** by Thomas B. Costain
53 **Kit Carson and the Wild Frontier** by Ralph Moody
54 **Robert E. Lee and the Road of Honor** by Hodding Carter
55 **Guadalcanal Diary** by Richard Tregaskis
56 **Commodore Perry and the Opening of Japan** by Ferdinand Kuhn
57 **Davy Crockett** by Stewart H. Holbrook
58 **Clara Barton, Founder of the American Red Cross** by Helen Dore Boylston
59 **The Story of San Francisco** by Charlotte Jackson
60 **Up the Trail from Texas** by J. Frank Dobie
61 **Abe Lincoln: Log Cabin to White House** by Sterling North
62 **The Story of D-Day: June 6, 1944** by Bruce Bliven, Jr.
63 **Rogers' Rangers and the French and Indian War** by Bradford Smith
64 **The World's Greatest Showman: The Life of P. T. Barnum** by J. Bryan III
65 **Sequoyah: Leader of the Cherokees** by Alice Marriott
66 **Ethan Allen and the Green Mountain Boys** by Slater Brown
67 **Wyatt Earp: U. S. Marshal** by Stewart H. Holbrook
68 **The Early Days of Automobiles** by Elizabeth Janeway
69 **The Witchcraft of Salem Village** by Shirley Jackson

70 The West Point Story
by Colonel Red Reeder & Nardi Reeder Campion

71 George Washington: Frontier Colonel
by Sterling North

72 The Texas Rangers
by Will Henry

73 Buffalo Bill's Great Wild West Show
by Walter Havighurst

74 Evangeline and the Acadians
by Robert Tallant

75 The Story of the Secret Service
by Ferdinand Kuhn

76 Tippecanoe and Tyler, Too!
by Stanley Young

77 America's First World War
by Henry Castor

78 The Doctors Who Conquered Yellow Fever by Ralph Nading Hill

79 Remember the Alamo!
by Robert Penn Warren

80 Andrew Carnegie and the Age of Steel
by Katherine B. Shippen

81 Geronimo: Wolf of the Warpath
by Ralph Moody

82 The Story of the Paratroops
by George Weller

83 The American Revolution
by Bruce Bliven, Jr.

84 The Story of the Naval Academy
by Felix Riesenberg, Jr.

85 Alexander Hamilton and Aaron Burr
by Anna Erskine Crouse and Russel Crouse

86 Stonewall Jackson
by Jonathan Daniels

87 The Battle for the Atlantic
by Jay Williams

88 The First Transatlantic Cable
by Adele Gutman Nathan

89 The Story of the Air Force
by Robert Loomis

90 Heroines of the Early West
by Nancy Wilson Ross

WORLD LANDMARK BOOKS

W-1 The First Men in the World
by Anne Terry White

W-2 Alexander the Great by John Gunther

W-3 Adventures and Discoveries of Marco Polo by Richard J. Walsh

W-4 Joan of Arc by Nancy Wilson Ross

W-5 King Arthur and His Knights
by Mabel L. Robinson

W-6 Mary, Queen of Scots by Emily Hahn

W-7 Napoleon and the Battle of Waterloo by Frances Winwar

W-8 Royal Canadian Mounted Police
by Richard L. Neuberger

W-9 The Man Who Changed China
by Pearl S. Buck

W-10 The Battle of Britain
by Quentin Reynolds

W-11 The Crusades by Anthony West

W-12 Genghis Khan and the Mongol Horde by Harold Lamb

W-13 Queen Elizabeth and the Spanish Armada by Frances Winwar

W-14 Simón Bolívar by Arnold Whitridge

W-15 The Slave Who Freed Haiti
by Katharine Scherman

W-16 The Story of Scotland Yard
by Laurence Thompson

W-17 The Life of Saint Patrick
by Quentin Reynolds

W-18 The Exploits of Xenophon
by Geoffrey Household

W-19 Captain Cook Explores the South Seas by Armstrong Sperry

W-20 Marie Antoinette by Bernardine Kielty

W-21 Will Shakespeare and the Globe Theater by Anne Terry White

W-22 The French Foreign Legion
by Wyatt Blassingame

W-23 Martin Luther by Harry Emerson Fosdick

W-24 The Hudson's Bay Company
by Richard Morenus

W-25 Balboa: Swordsman and Conquistador by Felix Riesenberg, Jr.

W-26 The Magna Charta by James Daugherty

W-27 Leonardo da Vinci by Emily Hahn

W-28 General Brock and Niagara Falls
by Samuel Hopkins Adams

W-29 Catherine the Great
by Katharine Scherman

W-30 The Fall of Constantinople
by Bernardine Kielty

W-31 Ferdinand Magellan
by Seymour Gates Pond

W-32 Garibaldi: Father of Modern Italy
by Marcia Davenport

W-33 The Story of Albert Schweitzer
by Anita Daniel

W-34 The Marquis de Lafayette: Bright Sword for Freedom by Hodding Carter

W-35 Famous Pirates of the New World
by A. B. C. Whipple

W-36 Exploring the Himalaya
by William O. Douglas

W-37 Queen Victoria by Noel Streatfeild

W-38 The Flight and Adventures of Charles II by Charles Norman

W-39 Chief of the Cossacks
by Harold Lamb

W-40 Adventures of Ulysses
by Gerald Gottlieb

W-41 William the Conqueror
by Thomas B. Costain

Landmark
BOOKS